The 360 Degree CEO

The 360 Degree CEO

Generating Profits While Leading and Living with Passion and Principles

Lorraine A. Moore

The 360 Degree CEO: Generating Profits While Leading and Living with Passion and Principles

Copyright © Business Expert Press, LLC, 2018.

First published in 2018 by
Business Expert Press, LLC
222 East 46th Street, New York, NY 10017
www.businessexpertpress.com

ISBN-13: 978-1-63157-517-4 (paperback)
ISBN-13: 978-1-63157-518-1 (e-book)

Business Expert Press Human Resource Management and Organizational Behavior Collection

Collection ISSN: 1946-5637 (print)
Collection ISSN: 1946-5645 (electronic)

Cover and interior design by Exeter Premedia Services Private Ltd., Chennai, India

First edition: 2018

10 9 8 7 6 5 4 3 2 1

Printed in the United States of America.

This book is dedicated to the executives who shared their stories and to my clients who place their trust in me and strive every day to become better leaders and people. Also, as always to my family who make this adventure called life, so fulfilling and joyful.

Abstract

The CEO and his/her leadership team are "on the job" at all times, expected to be available on a moment's notice. The term "24/7" is a reality to most of us and has blurred the separation between our personal and work lives.

This book provides an amalgamation of lessons from Moore's work with some of the best leaders in Fortune 1000 companies, privately held firms, mid-cap businesses, and not-for-profit organizations. Drawing on real-life examples from energy/oil and gas, financial services, professional services, world-class technology firms, mining, retail, healthcare, and more, Moore highlights the industry agnostic practices of both individual leaders and teams.

The 360 degree CEO provides the tools and insights to successfully navigate our personal and professional journeys, elevating our health, our relationships, our results, and our organization's performance.

Keywords

CEOs, energy/oil and gas, ethics, executive performance, financial services, improving results, integrity, leadership, leading change, managing change, managing teams, organizational change, regulation, strategy, team leadership, vision, work/life balance

Contents

CHAPTER 1

Purpose, Passion, and Principles (P³)

Purpose

An overarching purpose guides 360 degree CEOs. It may be grounded in personal interest in the industry—agriculture as it feeds the world, energy as it provides the life source for cities and homes to operate, healthcare as new treatments contribute to improved lives. Or the sense of purpose may be demonstrated in the leader's ability to create a raison d'etre for their employees, to define a vision or to highlight the context within which their work matters.

> *Right now, we are going through a restructuring going to public. To keep people motivated, inspired and engaged when the workloads are extraordinary is challenging. It's hard for people who have not been through that environment as I have more than once. It helps to maintain the vision of what comes out the other side, which is an extraordinarily large journey with a better balance and greater personal rewards in terms of accomplishment and generally, hopefully, rewards that make their lives better as well.*
>
> —Mayo Schmidt

Passion

360 degree CEOs are passionate about their work—and typically within their lives as well. They are so very good at what they do because they carry within them a fervor that energizes them when they face seemingly insurmountable challenges. And when their passion wanes, and that can happen to any of us, if it is not a short-lived dip, they change their circumstances. They return to something that energizes them again so that they can perform at their best.

When Ben Voss was appointed CEO of Morris Industries, he commented:

> Farming has always been very close to my heart. When we decided to purchase part of the farm from my parents a few years ago, it was really amazing to make that a key part of our lives. Now I also get to be part of one of the most iconic farm equipment companies in the world. As a farmer, as an engineer … pretty awesome.

> The job of a CEO is about courage; it's about listening to your management team, about listening to your board. And it's about having somebody you can run ideas past—your spouse, your chairmen, your mother, somebody you can be real with. You can't carry it all on your shoulders. In the end, CEOs must make the decisions. Give the team as big a sandbox as they can handle. When it works, it's a thing of beauty, it's worth all of that. It's exciting, and it's truly like the saying, love what you do and you will never work a day in your life. There are hurdles, yes, but if it's easy, anyone would do it.
>
> —Randy Findlay

> In 1995, I formed a company called Crestone International with two other partners and about a year later I became CEO of that company. Through organic growth, mergers and acquisitions we have been able to grow to about 2,000 employees in three different countries doing about $350M in revenue. It's been a fantastic ride, I've seen a lot of changes and I can't believe I've been at it for almost 21 years. It's really been fantastic.
>
> —Cal Yonker

Principles

Most highly successful CEOs combine their passion with a company that enables them to adhere to their principles.

I love the electricity industry and that's why I actually chose it when I had an opportunity to return to the gas business, because it's a lifeline business. And the electricity industry matters. You know it really matters. You know that without electricity we would not have the economies, the health and the people's livelihoods that are affected by electricity. And so, just by being in this industry, I find that quite rewarding because it really matters to people's lives. And so is being able to lead a company that takes that responsibility very seriously and always wants to be better and create that environment.

—Gianna Manes

In this book, I use CEO, senior leader, and leader interchangeably. This is intentional, as these principles are applicable and can be successfully applied to managers and leaders at all levels. It will be all the better if you adopt and apply these learnings before you reach the top spot or even if you do not aspire to it. By applying the attributes of a 360 degree CEO, you will be a more satisfied and well-rounded person and a better manager and leader for heeding the lessons herein. Some of my CEO clients run $3B companies; others lead $20M companies. The CEOs whose stories populate these pages are leading or have led companies of all sizes—from mid cap to Fortune 100. The principles in this book apply to leaders of all ages and genders across all industries, geographies, and sizes of company.

Enduring Characteristics that Generate Results

For the purposes of this book and to further my expertise in executive performance, I held conversations with CEOs from across North America. When approaching CEOs, I identified those who were broadly respected by their peers and communities, recommended by their executive teams and peers, and had demonstrated sustained financial performance. In several cases, these CEOs have also won awards from external bodies in recognition of their high standards of performance. The discussions were candid, vulnerable, and humble. All displayed passion for their work and were generous with their time.

So what constitutes a 360 degree CEO? From my research, interviews, and experience with thousands of CEOs, it is not easy to attain, but the formula is simple, powerful, and achievable.

360 degree CEOs demonstrate P³. They generate profits by leading with… Purpose, Passion, and Principles.

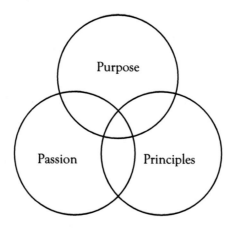

The powerful trifecta: Purpose, Passion, and Principles (P³)

Purpose, Passion, and Principles (P³)

Purpose

Leaders who demonstrate **purpose** express their "why" in a way that excites and inspires their employees. Decades of research have reaffirmed that most people want to make a difference at work; they want to believe that what they do really matters and makes a difference in the world. When the CEO and other leaders offer a sense of purpose and loftier goals than profits and employment, employees respond. And here is a tip—in my interactions with those I consider 360 degree leaders, they are passionate when they describe the purpose of their organization. It is not enough to be able to describe the greater good or the overarching benefits to stakeholders—they have to still care about it.

Some of their comments are as follows:

- "Our products improve the day to day lives of our customers and their families."

- "Our company creates interesting work and a great livelihood for thousands of people."
- "We're providing energy that powers lives."—Mayo Schmidt
- "The electricity industry really matters. Without it, we would not have our economies and people's health and livelihoods… It really matters to people's lives"—Gianna Manes
- "We have a Rhodes Scholar in our band. We intervene when there are drugs. We are creating a better future for our band."—Rose Laboucan
- "We help save lives."
- "We are changing the face of education."

When I spoke with Mayo Schmidt, President and CEO of Hydro One, he shared how a sense of purpose can help navigate through very demanding times in our careers.

Right now we're going through a reorganization of a company, moving from crown into public [it is challenging] to keep people motivated, inspired, and engaged. The workloads are extraordinary right now and it's hard for people who haven't been through this environment more than once, as I have. It helps to maintain the vision of what comes out the other side, which is an extraordinarily large journey with a better balance and greater personal rewards in terms of accomplishments and, hopefully, rewards that make their lives better as well.

Passion

Leaders exhibiting **passion** speak with **energy and conviction**.

- "I get excited about creating winning teams."
- "This is a fascinating industry that is always evolving. Technology is going to revolutionize healthcare and I want to be part of it."

Passionate leaders retain enthusiasm even in challenging environments. They are not cheerleaders. They are not eternal optimists. They have conviction and fervor, oftentimes displayed as a quiet and confident energy. They care about what they are doing. They care about the company, the customers, and the purpose in a way that sustains them and others through periods of growth and downturns. They are in the industry or at the company that they are by choice. It is where they want to be; it aligns to their interests, their strengths, and their experiences. This is not to say they never lose their passion. But when that happens, they move on and seek a situation in which they can be mostly fulfilled and lead with passion (more on that in a later chapter).

In addition to being known for operating with the highest integrity, Gianna Manes demonstrates passion in every conversation, speech, and interaction:

> Being a CEO allows me to affect an entire culture. That's what gives me the most satisfaction and fulfillment. One of my biggest responsibilities is to create an environment where people can bring out their best and the collective best. Then we all align and point in the right direction. The leaders in this organization need to be of that ilk and that's the environment I want to create and it starts from the top. That's what I really love doing.

Principles

Principled leaders make decisions and take action based on a **core set of values**. They do not alter their decisions or the course of the company. I expect that most of us can cite examples in which this was not the case, as those are often identified in the media. This is what sets principled leaders apart.

- "I have certain beliefs and a set of values that are important to me. At times I had to compromise to some extent, but never to the point that I couldn't sleep at night."
- "Doing business in other countries… the normal protocol was to violate certain principles to get business done and we would just simply not do that. So, I think you're called out all the time to make decisions that you have to reach in to yourself and ask, what's the right thing to do?"

Everybody's got integrity until it gets tested in some way. Your integrity is tested when you have to take out your chequebook to write a cheque. If you are willing to pay for your decision, you know you've got integrity. [As the CEO of a law firm and a non-lawyer] there were people who liked my approach and a lot of people who didn't. There were people who wanted to be let off the hook; I had a line that I was not prepared to cross. When I was younger, I was far more black and white, and as I've gotten older, the grey zone has increased. It's not as cut and dried as when I was younger. I have run every business the same way. I can walk down the street and if I run into someone whom I've fired, I can speak with him or her. I do not have to cross the street and walk the other way.

—Geoff Pulford

Some CEOs have said that it became harder to stay true to their values as they took on more senior roles. When I posed this question to Ed Clark, former CEO of TD Bank Financial Group, he responded:

I haven't found that. Firstly, you've had more successes, so you're more self-confident when you've gone with your gut again against the market to do the right thing... you're good. You're trying to run an organization in the long run and people want to feel proud of that organization. You should be trying to build an organization that 10 or 15 years later people will say, "This is a great place. I've made the right decisions at the right time." I've actually found that it's easier to [stay aligned to my values when you see what happens to] people who make short-term decisions and sacrifice the long term. It makes you more self-confident in saying, "we should do the right thing and we should do the right thing for 10 years from now." The job of a CEO at a bank is to have a vision and show where you can get growth and lead that growth, but it's equally being prepared to say no against opposition, not just outside the company, but inside the company as well.

Swiss Re's former CEO balances passion and principles:

> Swiss Re doesn't just care about profitability. They want to create a better environment and make the world a better place. Swiss Re is very, very special in terms of its ability to influence the world.
>
> For example, they spend a lot of time trying to help develop better water filtration in countries where not having clean water is the one thing that will wipe out the population. They invest enormous amounts of financial and human resources in creating solutions with governments around the world. They don't have to do this. They could simply be a reinsurance company. The Swiss Re CEO says: "We are a research engine with a reinsurer bolted on to the back end." All of Swiss Re's country CEOs have passion about "how do you make the world a better place?" Being in the top 10 most sustainable companies in corporate social responsibility is brought to life because of and through the decisions and the actions of the CEO.
>
> —Sharon Ludlow

To be fully engaged as a high-performing leader, you need to exercise all three of these traits: purpose, passion, and principles. It is not always easy. Passion will wane. Your principles will be tested. Identifying when one of the core attributes is missing or lessened and then taking action to address this will put you in good stead in the long run.

Purpose + Passion – Principles = Lack of integrity
Passion + Principles – Purpose = No destination, no inspiring rallying cry
Purpose + Principles – Passion = Going through the motions, opportunity cost to you and the company.

Embracing All Facets of Your Life

It is a warm day at the beach. Envision a cloudless blue sky and a stretch of calm lake water extending out in front of you. In the distance a sailboat seemingly glides across your line of sight. The sails are full, the spinnaker a rainbow of colors. When the sails in your life are filled through living a life of authenticity, with confidence, robust health, and vulnerability, you too can attain grace in calm waters and better navigate the storms that arise in every life.

360 degree CEOs attend to all aspects of their lives—not just work. They are multidimensional with broad and varied interests. This is part of what makes them such interesting, as well as successful and highly respected, people. We will explore this further in Chapter 9 where we review the traits of the new giants.

Relationships

360 degree CEOs place a high value on relationships, particularly with family.

> There are certain things that you never want to delegate. Time and schedule are something that I don't delegate to an assistant. It's probably not the most efficient but I find it's more effective to control my own calendar because that's my time and I don't want to lose control of it. I go through annual, monthly and weekly planning sessions by myself and make sure as part of those planning sessions I am blocking large chunks of time for the priorities and goals I have. Whether that's as a husband, as a family man, my friends or social, self-development; and also, of course, work. So, I view it as an entire package and I like how you phrase it as "whole life" versus work/life balance. Many people ask me about work/life balance, but to me work and sleep are both part of life so why don't we talk about work/sleep balance? I just view it all as life balance. The first part is owning my own calendar and I make the decisions as to where my time goes as part of that. The second part is how do you leverage the time you have to accomplish many of your goals. So for example, with regards to my wife, we both love to train for triathlons and we do that together on weekends as well as going to events. My daughter has gotten into it so we have added her to that training as well. After training my son joins us and we rotate cooking assignments so we have fun making

each other meals. In just a few hours I can accomplish goals with regards to my wife, my family and love of cooking. So a lot of it is just in the planning and making sure that you're doing things together that everyone likes and can enjoy together. Owning your time and then making sure you are planning out the activities, that they get on your calendar in big blocks of time and then not letting ANYTHING interfere with that.

—Cal Yonker

It struck me that virtually all of the CEOs I spoke with reflected on the values they learned from their parents, the respect they had for their parents, and/or were in a long-term relationship with a spouse (sometimes a second marriage). This sampling is not statistically reliable or valid but I believe there is a correlation.

Hal Kvisle spoke with quiet reverence about his father who came from Norway and was a remarkable outdoorsman, a biologist by training, and a teacher by income. Hal recounted summer outdoors with his father and the lifelong love for the outdoors that it created in Hal. His mother's family homesteaded and pioneered in Alberta in 1895. Hal described his "rudimentary dwelling in rugged foothills country, heated by wood with no running water as a fun place to go," and a place that he has shared many happy hours with his children. When spending time there, Hal can relate to his grandfather as a 17-year-old boy, building a sod house in order to survive the harsh winter with no money and few supplies. Hal spoke of having "driven these values home to his kids" as well as the love of skiing that his father demonstrated. "People need to stay connected with where they come from and not get obsessed about where they want to go."

My parents believed in dreaming and then dreaming big and accomplishing those dreams and never at any time dashing those dreams by saying that there was anything that you set your mind to that you couldn't do.

—Mayo Schmidt

Executives with a partner who supports them in their considerable work demands (emotionally and with practical items at home) and who offers counsel, and at times a contrary view, may have a greater ability to sustain a 360 degree balance. There is considerable research correlating marriage with a longer life expectancy. I am not suggesting that a spouse is required to achieve the success of the CEOs herein but it does indicate some potential benefits.

Rose Laboucan spent most of her time away from home and family. Her husband, also a Chief, shouldered most of the responsibility at home and with the children while she was on the road, attending meetings in Ottawa with politicians, with band members across Alberta, and with other chiefs. As with all of the leaders in this book, the travel and time away from home is not easy for anyone. But I think in particular the support that Rose's spouse demonstrated to her was particularly unique for a male in an Aboriginal community. He placed his wife's career ahead of his own role as a Chief. He received some negative feedback from others for doing this but stayed the course and was committed to his values.

Home is a place of balance for me and having a spouse who creates that environment is a godsend.

—Cal Yonker

We were once buying a new bed and my wife said, "I don't know why we need a new bed. In 25 years, your side has only been slept on for 10 years."

—Brian MacNeill

Mayo Schmidt raised his daughters, on his own, for well over a decade while occupying very demanding leadership roles such as the CEO of Viterra and Hydro. "I made a commitment early on with my two daughters that they were going to be my priority in life," said Schmidt. "As much as work is absolutely a dedication and [requires] commitment, I wouldn't put either my family, which is first, or my health which is second to that (but it is important because it serves the purpose of the first), at risk for a career opportunity. Fortunately we are not or should not be asked to put those two things at risk. However, we are often distracted by significant events in our work lives and that creates a situation or outcome where it is difficult to be present. I try and get engaged and do things that they're passionate about so that we can do things together. I started that when they were young whether it was taking my daughters walking, jogging, kayaking, or mountain climbing. I tried to make it outdoors and physical and then the circumstances created an engagement. It's easy to lose the connection. It's easy to not be present mentally but be there physically."

Sometimes even 360 degree CEOs fall short; we all do. Luc Desjardins, CEO and President Superior Plus, shared how one of his decisions impacted his family. While his youngest daughter was in university, his work involved him relocating thousands of miles away. He expected that there would be minimal impact on his family and that his daughter would be comfortable with her parents living so far away. She was not comfortable having her parents so far away, so his wife stayed in their home city, while his daughter completed university. He shared his regret over this situation, as he felt that his work choice had been difficult for his family.

CHAPTER 2

The Business Case for the Whole CEO

Energy management boils down to three things: sleep, diet, exercise. The common process goes back to making sure you have the right routine, the right discipline to make sure those three stay in sync. I think there is a direct link between those three things and passion. They drive energy and it's hard to be passionate about anything when you lack the energy. I find as I get older energy management becomes a larger issue than it was in my 20–30s.

—Cal Yonker

360 degree CEOs deliver sustained shareholder value. They propel organizations through economic downturns, fortuitous acquisitions, strong financial tail winds, and unexpected public or internal mistakes. 360 degree leaders do not mistake their worth or their capability as being defined by the stock price and, therefore, rely on judgment, experience, and the counsel of others when making strategic choices. This chapter uses examples to demonstrate the shareholder benefits of the 360 degree CEO, and the most important traits identified by corporate boards.

Financial success is an outcome of doing a lot of other things well—people misunderstand that to be that it's not important or that I'm diminishing its importance and it's not that. So I am careful how I emphasize that, because certain people struggle and I still have many people who will say "well you're here to turn a profit for your shareholder." Yes, our shareholder value proposition very clearly states in the first words that we provide a stable, steady growing dividend and have long term growth value and growth of the organization/enterprise. But we also list four other things that focus on how we're going to do it and it's those other things that I try to focus the organization around executing.

—Gianna Manes

Results Right to the Bottom Line

Commencing in 2010, *Harvard Business Review* has evaluated chief executives' financial performance over their entire tenure in office. In 2013, they added performance in the area of corporate social responsibility and evaluated a global pool of over 3,100 CEOs. The top CEOs on their list performed in the stratosphere. On average, the top 100 executives on their list delivered total shareholder return of 1,385 percent during their tenures and increased the market value of their companies by $40.2 billion (including adjustments for inflation, dividends, share repurchases, and share issues). In contrast, for the 100 executives on the bottom of the list, total shareholder returns were –57 percent and the companies experienced a cumulative decline in market value of $13.6 billion.

https://hbr.org/2013/01/the-best-performing-ceos-in-the-world

In this chapter we explore some more of the practices of 360 degree CEOs. These include leadership athleticism, integrity, risk taking, and more.

Leadership athleticism is comprised of a set of characteristics and behaviors that I previously identified through my work with senior clients. Executives demonstrating leadership athleticism recognize and acknowledge that their jobs are demanding—physically, mentally, and emotionally—and consistently make the choices and sacrifices that are required to sustain 360 degree performance over the long term. But what does this look like?

Preparing for the Physical Demands

Executives lead demanding lives. Travel and long workdays may be common elements of their jobs. Changing time zones, unfamiliar hotel beds, fast food, alcohol, rich meals, sedentary periods on planes, and long car and train rides, all take a toll on one's physical stamina and overall wellness. When we are fatigued and/or away from our regular surroundings, we are more likely to forgo the habits of healthy eating, exercise, and adequate sleep. Everyone knows this. The difference is that high-performing executives demonstrate a commitment to sustained health. In some cases, they are motivated by having experienced ill health or have seen the effects in others. On occasion, they were athletes during university and have maintained a commitment to sport and fitness. Every executive with a disciplined health regime acknowledges the positive effects on stress and mental acuity.

Cal Yonker reflected and shared:

Passion requires sleep, diet and exercise. You can't have passion without good energy. As I get older, energy management becomes a much larger issue than in my 20s and 30s. If my passion wanes, it generally occurs when things are running well and my team is out executing. In those situations I find myself getting a bit bored and less passionate about the business. This was a surprising revelation that I had.

Fred Tomczyk, former CEO of TD Ameritrade, schedules meetings for 9 a.m. or later whenever possible. This ensures that he is able to complete a 30–45 minute workout every day. As he described it, he knows that when he arrives at the office, his day is not his own; he is expected to be physically and mentally present and attentive. He recognizes the necessity of dedicating time to preserving his health, not just in the immediate term, that is, avoiding the common cold, but also for the long term.

Your work situation may not allow for a 9 a.m. start. Or, like me, you may find it difficult to commit to a morning exercise routine. There is no reason to forgo an exercise program. When I had young, school-aged children in addition to my demanding full-time jobs, I worked out over my lunch hour at least three times per week. For a period of time, I went to a gym. Other times, I put a pair of roller blades in the trunk of my car or running gear in my desk drawer. When I could not fit exercise into the busy mornings or evenings, I used the time that I could.

> When I interviewed Luc Desjardins, he had recently completed a 25 km fundraising walk with employees of Hydro One and, following the organized event, returned home by walking an additional 6 km. It is no coincidence that in his 50s, with scores of successful acquisitions to his name, he retains the energy and stamina to passionately transform a company of over 5,000 employees with $15B in market cap. We share a love of fine wine and good food and yet Luc is selective in what he eats and limits his alcohol intake to ensure that he stays at the top of his game.

Neuroscientists would support Fred and Luc's choices. Our brain represents about 2 percent of our body weight, yet utilizes 25 percent of the energy we consume through the food we eat, including 70 percent of our glucose intake. If you want to be a highly successful leader, recognized for making astute decisions, managing ambiguity, handling crises, and being able to process large quantities of often-contradictory information, you need to support your brain with an intake of healthy foods as well as adequate sleep and movement.

The research is endless on the effects of stress and lifestyle. Prolonged stress, poor nutrition, inadequate sleep, and inactivity increase our susceptibility to strokes, heart attack, cancer, and so on. Fred's experience is that in order to perform at a peak mental capacity, exercise the best judgment, effectively manage inevitable stressors, and enable his body to resist the negative effects of travel, jet lag, long hours, and changing time zones, he must prioritize his health. Neuroscientists would agree.

Making Health and Wellness a Priority

What differentiates 360 degree CEOs from other leaders is that they consistently heed the evidence. They do not delay making the required changes, nor do they discard their health regimes until the next quarter, following completion of the M&A, and so on. They schedule the time. They sacrifice time suckers that others do not—social media, television, easy, fast food meals while traveling, high caloric food at business dinners, or that second or third glass of wine. This is how they are able to hold CEO positions for multiple years, sometimes for multiple companies. They provide the fuel for their bodies (food, exercise, and rest), which fuels their minds.

In Isaccson's biography of Steve Jobs, the author relays that Jobs attributed the spread of cancer, in part, to being physically fatigued for a period of time. While he was running Apple and still working at Pixar, Jobs spoke of being so tired when he returned home in the evenings that he did not physically have the energy to speak with his wife, Laurene. He believed this lessened his body's ability to fight the disease.

Discipline and Tenacity

In my experience, these characteristics are often linked. Merriam-Webster defines discipline as an "orderly or prescribed conduct or pattern of behavior" and tenacious as "persistent in maintaining, adhering to, or seeking something valued or desired." The latter qualifier is particularly interesting to me. Tenacity is not adherence to every goal, to every action, to every decision, but rather to those outcomes that are truly valued or desired. This prioritization and selection is one of the secrets to becoming a 360 degree CEO. These successful leaders persevere when attending to their most important goals. If you similarly differentiate your goals and activities, it will free up time and capacity to enable you to attend to the outcomes that really matter.

Mastering Your Day

Early in my career, I was fortunate to meet Merv Lahn, CEO of Canada Trust. One day in my mid-20s, I asked him how he juggled the multiple demands on his time. He gave me two tips: he relied on a fantastic executive assistant, Norma McBurney, and he only touched each piece of incoming mail or reading material one time. Immediately after reading a memo he would take action, file it, or respond. He never set something aside to be dealt with later. Imagine if we followed this with our e-mail as well as hard copy information. While you may not institute Merv's practice, the following exercise is equally effective and powerful, particularly when followed consistently.

Exercise #1—Mastering Your Day

Every morning before you do anything else in the office—check voicemail, read e-mail, stop by someone's office to ask about their weekend …

- Write down the six things you would want to accomplish, even if you completed nothing else during your day.
- Take action.
- Complete these six tasks before you do anything else.

My clients' lists have included: call Customer A and B; arrange medical appointment; prepare for Board meeting; schedule a difficult conversation with a colleague; set a date for a planning session; or review the most recent sales report.

If your current practice is to arrive at the office and immediately jump into meetings and activity, you have a few options:

- Create your list every evening for the next day.
- Create your list before you leave the house.
- Arrive earlier to the office.
- Block off 30 to 45 minutes in your calendar every day— first thing—to action these items.

What you will discover is that these six items are typically ones with longer-term benefits: to your health; to relationships with others; to refreshing your leadership capabilities; to your company's brand; or to raising the bar on your performance. They are frequently priorities that are small but powerful.

> The time required to complete them will vary; sometimes it's an hour, sometimes as long as two hours, depending on your most important priorities at the time. I expect you will find, like others have, that most days you will knock off these tasks in less than 30 minutes. If you have a large, and potentially daunting, project in front of you—use one of your six tasks to schedule blocks of time in your calendar to work on the large project.

Building Upon Your Natural Rhythms

Where are you most disciplined? Maintaining a healthy diet and consistent fitness regime as described earlier are obviously examples of discipline. Another example is the executive who consistently meets up with his friends for men's hockey league or the woman who carves out time to attend her book club. One of the most beneficial habits can be weekend dinners with family, as the rush of the activities during the week heavily impinge on our ability to stay connected with our spouse and children. One of my clients adopted a practice of calling his wife every day at 4 p.m. to check in and let her know when he expected to be home. While he still works long days and often arrives home after 7 p.m., his wife now feels more respected and is thus more supportive of his work demands.

Another example of discipline is consistently taking one's allocated vacation. Many North American executives do not take their entitled vacation, nor do their employees. We have purposefully or unconsciously created a culture that espouses long hours at the office and little or no time off. In some cases, this was viewed as a boon to productivity. It is not. It contributes to declining employee engagement, increased incidents of internal fraud, lower productivity, and lessened mental and physical health and stamina.

In the United States, there is no government requirement for employers to provide any paid vacation days. In Canada and Japan, the government mandates 10 days of paid vacation. In Australia, Belgium, New Zealand, and the Netherlands, the government mandates 20 days. In Germany it is 24 and in Finland and Sweden it is 25. France is the highest with 30 days. Not surprisingly, when I spoke with executives in Europe and Asia, they are more likely to take their holidays and state the importance of taking a mental break from the workplace.

The Demanding Workplace

It can be very challenging for CEOs to take time away from the office, particularly during an acquisition phase, while navigating challenging discussions with shareholders or regulators, and so on. However, this is exactly when you and your team will receive the greatest benefit from your absence. Time away from the office will provide you with perspective. Work is not your entire life, even though it may be a most significant part of your life (just ask anyone who has been diagnosed with a serious illness). In your absence, you will delegate responsibility to others who will benefit from independently addressing new challenges. Your team will benefit from problem solving and even taking the lead on responding to a crisis when they are required to do so without your oversight. You want your management team and their employees to take their holidays. The company performance and financial results will be stronger and these are measures of your performance. Communicating the benefits to your management team is not sufficient. As in all ways, you must model the behavior you seek from others.

Finally, you will make better decisions, live a richer and fuller life, enjoy stronger relationships, and extend your life expectancy.

Paul Kelly, President and CEO, First Calgary and Connect First, discussed a time that there was a very important meeting scheduled at the same time that his father was scheduled to visit from across the country. There were seven other attendees, all with equally demanding schedules and all of whom were able to make it that particular week but could not make it the week before or the week following. Many CEOs would have taken time away from the family visit to attend the meeting or as Paul suggested, would have made an excuse that his absence would be attributable to another business requirement. He indicated that many would be afraid to be honest about making a commitment to family or other personal commitments over an important work event.

If you have worked steadily for two or three years without taking more than a few days holidays, why is this? The most common responses are:

- "We recently completed merger or other organizational transformation."
- "I have many new members on the management team."
- "New board members or a new board chair are asking for information and asking questions and are seeking much of my available time."
- "I have been in this role less than 3 years and I have been full on."

These are all logical, but that is the problem. This logic lets you off the hook. It feeds your ego. Here is a tip for you: if a manager is not taking their holidays, or only takes his or her holidays when you are also away, this is often an indicator of insecurity. In these cases, they may lack confidence and worry that in their absence someone else will step in and perform the job better than they do or you will discover something they are not doing as well as you expected. In other cases, the individual has allotted so much of their life to work that they have no interests and few satisfying relationships outside of the office.

Now consider yourself. If you are not taking holidays or time away from the office, reach deeper than your first explanations and consider: are you using work as a refuge from a lonely personal life? Do you lack confidence in your team to lead the company or division in your absence? What else might be holding you back from taking time away?

Sometimes it is completely legitimate. You took on the role 20 months prior and discovered more issues than you anticipated. You have spent weeks traveling across the country for employee town halls and customer meetings. Perhaps you and your CFO have also been securing financing or running a large project such as an ERP (enterprise resource planning system) and implementation has been much more difficult than expected. This has been the case with some of my best clients and highest performing CEOs. If this describes your situation, I understand. And if you are my client, I am asking you to pull out your calendar and schedule your next holiday.

Integrity at Work

Enron, Wells Fargo employees opening false bank accounts, Fannie Mae and Freddie Mac, Valeant's exorbitant price hike for Cuprine and other pharmaceutical drugs and other widely known corporate scandals and greed-driven actions have contributed to a loss of confidence in corporate North America. When interviewing CEOs for this book, I asked them to comment on the media's portrayal of our loss of heroes and heroines. Their responses did not surprise me and were consistent with the attributes of 360 degree CEOs. Most acknowledged that citizens' concerns were justified. However, as a counter, many commented that there are numerous examples of everyday heroes and heroines around the world. We just need to look in our own neighborhoods and communities.

A highly respected board chair recounted a situation from when he was CEO. A large customer overpaid an invoice to his firm by over $1 million. When the CFO identified this, the top leader immediately instructed that the money be returned to the customer. Not everyone agreed that they should proceed so rapidly. Some felt there was little harm in retaining the money. This 360 degree leader acknowledged that while he has many flaws, he will never sacrifice his integrity. He lives by the belief that when you do the right thing and when you make honorable choices, your company will be more profitable and you will be more successful and wealthier over time. In his words, "to some, it may not appear this way in the short term, but in the long run, integrity always wins and one always benefits." In addition to demonstrating integrity, his comments demonstrate another characteristic of 360 executives—self-awareness.

Sometimes leaders demonstrate their integrity to the greatest extent when supporting their employees.

One of my healthcare clients experienced a year of disappointing financial results. A promising new product did not deliver the expected sales in spite of effective market research, marketing, distribution, and so on. All employees' incentive compensation was linked to corporate results; bonuses were calculated with a factor for EBITDA. Everyone would be impacted by the substandard performance. While the CEO and board were, and remain today, fully supportive of this compensation model, the CEO did not feel comfortable with all employees being negatively impacted by something that was largely out of their control.

The CEO proposed to the board that although executive team compensation carried the greatest weighting for corporate performance, it be even more heavily weighted for the prior year's performance. Those closest to the top of the organization and with the authority, ability, and responsibility to make strategic decisions would receive the greatest negative impact to their bonuses. The lower an employee resided in the organizational hierarchy, the less his or her bonus would be affected that year. The board agreed. The CEO communicated: "The closer you are to the top of the organization, the more you will pay for decisions or actions that have negative consequences." While this decision was not popular with all management, it resulted in deeper and more sustained employee commitment than had ever existed in the company. Realistically, while a smaller bonus may have created strain for some of the leadership team, the bulk of the work was and is completed by the majority of employees populating roles in customer service, regulatory and compliance, information services, research and development, and so on.

Communicate to employees. They should feel empowered to have a voice that says "I have a concern about this and here is why" and never feel like they will be questioned, particularly when applying [our] values to a circumstance. It's really about articulating the values and making employees feel safe to have a conversation that says "this is not right in the organization." [When someone breaks values, for leaders, it doesn't matter if you] didn't know or if someone else was condoning it. Neither is an excuse because even if one trader in a commodity business that you have never met does something wrong the question will always be, "did you have the right protocol, structure and values in place? Did you communicate those broadly enough that people felt that they didn't have to do things that weren't aligned with your values."

—Mayo Schmidt

Integrity in Every Aspect of Life

For the 360 degree executive, integrity extends beyond the workplace. It is reflected in who we are and the choices we make each and every day. Every executive I interviewed acknowledged the irrefutable requirement to consistently act in alignment with their personal values and beliefs and their stated priorities and commitments. They attributed their parents as having instilled values of honesty and ethical behavior in them and they wanted to carry that forward in their own lives.

My father was a mentor and, literally, a teacher. He was an inspiring guy and lived a strong set of values. In his 80s, he is still constantly moving, still farming, raising horses, going to the gym 6 days a week. So that motion is natural to me.

I've spent 14 years of my life on my own raising my daughters. Being in a leadership role there were penalties and benefits. The penalties were that there is a lot of responsibility. The benefit is you can, to a great degree, affect your schedule. I made a commitment early on with my two daughters that they were going to be my priority in life. As much as work is absolutely a dedication and commitment that we all have and achieving the maximum that we all can, I would not put my family or my health, which serves the purpose of the first, at risk for a career opportunity. Fortunately, we are not or should not be asked to put those first two things at risk.

However, we are often distracted by significant events in our work lives that create a situation or outcome where we find ourselves struggling to be present. Lack of personal time and lack of being present are penalties of leadership and that goes to self-sacrifice. That needs to be balanced. It can't go one way or the other. Most of life is balance. Trying to have that unique balance.

—Mayo Schmidt

Randy Findlay, Chairman of Pembina Pipeline and now a very proud grandfather, described juggling career and family commitments. He coached his sons' sports teams, actively participated in his children's daily lives and thought he had struck an optimal balance. So it was a surprise to him when one of his sons told him:

It's like we are all sitting around the campfire and we are all singing and trading stories and you are there dad but it's like you are in an outer circle, you're one circle back from being in the inner circle. We see you but we don't think you are actually participating and listening all the time.

Considering quality versus time was a big wakeup call. As an engineer, if there is something going on, "well let's talk about it" and then you go right for a solution. And they don't want solutions. They just want you to listen.

After his initial surprise at this disconnect, Randy made adjustments to close the gap.

Cal Yonker shared, "My wife will say 'you are not listening to me, right? Your head is somewhere else.' She will call me on it and I will say 'you are exactly right and let me see if I can reset and be here with you.' It definitely happens."

Many years ago, I attended a retirement party for Frank Pratt. He was a brilliantly creative marketing genius and taskmaster with a keen attention to detail. He had a successful career and was highly regarded. His legacy at retirement was a message to all of us still working—do not neglect your family. Your work is exhilarating and interesting, rewarding and prestigious, but as exciting as it is and as long a road as it seems, the journey will fairly rapidly come to an end and if you have not invested in your relationships with family and friends, you may have little waiting for you at the end of that road.

We all know but sometimes forget that being in physical proximity is not synonymous with being emotionally present. Most of us have done this—spent the weekend with the family at the cottage or attended the soccer tournament, patting ourselves on the back for being there but spending time with our heads bent over our smartphones responding to perceived urgent e-mails or lost in thought and not active in conversations. When we truly have integrity, it is reflected not just in our decisions at work but also in our interactions with friends and family.

Risk Taking

> I don't think there are enough CEOs that have the confidence to listen to their gut and the managerial courage to stand up and say you know 'no this isn't the right thing' or 'I don't believe in this.' When Jack Welch started as CEO…they lost a billion dollars within 24 months. Now he was lucky the COO kept him and then you know the rest of his career but it started with a big blow up.
>
> —Luc Desjardins

Most successful executives can point to examples of risks they took throughout their careers. Fred Tomczyk, CEO, TD Ameritrade, was enjoying a successful career in finance and expected to grow his career to become a CFO. A respected executive and mentor encouraged Fred to expand his career outside of finance, to acquire general management skills and to target a leadership position as a COO or CEO. Fred loved accounting and finance and knew he could be successful in that realm. He chose to take the risk of stepping into a different line of business and testing his skills in those areas.

"I ask myself… What's the worst thing that can happen? What's the downside? What do I have to lose? I remember sitting in the airport after being interviewed by the board and offered the job at Enmax; I was speaking with a dear friend on the phone. (Like many of us, Gianna Manes stared into the future of 'what ifs.' Accepting the role would mean moving her family from North Carolina and leaving a job she liked.) I asked my friend, "what if I don't like it? She responded, 'If it doesn't work out, you can leave.' It was a great reminder that we have choices. Don't be afraid of them. If they work, great. If they don't, well, that is ok too."

Risk taking applies to taking well-thought-out personal risks and enabling risk taking with your teams.

> We had this experience where we were going to replace a compressor. With our team concept, the gas plant team had lot of power and a lot of decision-making. Our engineering group recommended one type of compressor and our plant group said "we would like to try this other type of compressor." They grumbled, and said "fine." I said "No, no. If we force this on them it will never work." We went to see them 6 weeks after they got the compressor. They said, "yes it's great." Then when we were sitting down having coffee they said, "You know we had to work night and day to make this work and we didn't bill the company for the overtime because we knew we had chosen it and we had to find a way to make it work and we had a budget and we were not going to go over it." I just thought, "wow you guys have done it!" That's stepping out and allowing, and there was a fair amount at stake. Those are exciting and rewarding times. After that, if you asked them to walk off the face of the earth they would. Because they believed in the company and they believed in you.
>
> —Randy Findlay

CIOs and Risk

By the very nature of their responsibilities, CIOs and CFOs often shepherd initiatives that offer considerable risk to an organization. CFOs typically report directly to the CEO but this is not always the case for the

CIO. Because of this, ensuring that you have a highly functioning CIO who is much more than a technologist is very important. For purposes of this book and the discussion on risk, we will explore more about the role and contribution of the CIO.

I have had the opportunity to work with many CIOs. By far, the most successful CIOs are those who are business people first. In most cases, strategic, business-focused CIOs have held positions outside of the technology realm, sometimes in marketing or sales or having led a division with P&L responsibility. When leading other functions, they and their teams have been the beneficiaries of technology decisions and may have first-hand experience with the customer experience. This knowledge and any accompanying empathy equip these CIOs with the tools they need to make better leadership decisions. The interesting and perhaps often unseen connection is this—career technologists, CIOs who have worked in a variety of roles or have worked for different organizations, have taken a calculated risk during their career. They selected or were placed in a situation in which they stepped outside their comfort zone—moved to a different company or accepted a role in a different business discipline or industry. Owing, in part, to their success in navigating these transitions, they are often more comfortable assessing and taking appropriate risks as part of their executive role.

Technology is pervasive and often ubiquitous (more on this in Chapter 9, Traits of the New Giants). It also must be managed carefully to ensure that company and customer information is secure, to operate safety sensitive functions for airlines, pipelines, and so on. Boards are paying closer attention to technology risks and CIOs with broad business experience and strategic thinking capabilities are best positioned to lead this important area. So it is with CEOs and other C-suite positions. Experience in taking risk, even when the outcomes may not be as favorable as hoped, is fundamentally valuable.

Sharon Ludlow recounts how they changed their internal processes to better leverage technology. It is also a great example of risk management and decision making.

The organization needed to dramatically improve its digital capabilities in its customer service area in a very short period of time. That required not just investment in technology, but also to consider innovative ways for the organization to interact with its customers.

Customer service was traditionally provided over the phone, then email was introduced and now it has evolved to live chat and text as a method of interaction. The next evolution is virtual service and artificial intelligence whereby the customer shares photographs taken live at the scene of an accident and the insurance claims are adjudicated virtually. That's the kind of innovation we were striving for.

At the start of our project, we recruited subject matter experts in the insurance process. We assembled our team of insurance experts and challenged them to design the customer interaction. The problem was, these people knew a lot about insurance but they didn't know a lot about how to make that a fabulous customer experience.

We didn't look outside and ask, 'Who are the experts at excellent customer interaction?' Of course, one of the companies that is known for its excellent customer experience is Amazon. When you want to buy something, you can find it quickly, you can pay for it quickly, and it gets delivered quickly.

We didn't consider the customer experience initially, and as a result, we started to design something that we soon realized wasn't going to meet our expectations. So I made the decision to stop until we found the right expertise on how to create the best customer experience.

The organization's reaction was interesting. While stopping a project midstream isn't usually seen as a positive, the organization embraced it as an example of the agile way of working where initiatives are routinely tested, fail fast, and iterate. We needed the organization as a whole to start to learn how to operate in an agile way.

'Build a minimum viable product, not the Cadillac but the Chevy. Fail fast, throw it away.' We provided agile training to our entire team; and added external experts on customer experience to round out our strengths. Then we continued our work with a much better perspective; aimed at a much better solution.

When you dissect it as a business case we started down a path, we saw this wasn't going to work, we had the courage to stop. And then we created the right environment, said that it was OK to fail and then allowed people to carry on, and so in doing that the innovation part became quite clear. People were no longer afraid to suggest a new idea, they would say, 'let's try it.'

The agile way of working allowed teams to create, test and discard ideas quickly. We embarked on something that was very different for the organization and even in the early days I could see the excitement, enthusiasm and momentum from the leaders who were excited about this opportunity.

—Sharon Ludlow

Risk taking is not limited to personal career risk but includes making decisions for the long term, even when, and especially when, these choices may have negative implications in the short term. While leading TD Canada Trust, Ed Clark said no to offering mortgage-backed securities in spite of considerable opposition within the bank and against the tidal wave of products being offered by competitors. Had Ed supported the sale of these products, revenues would likely have been higher for a few financial reporting periods—but not over the long term.

When Luc Desjardins joined Superior, it was a crisis situation. Swimming in debt they were leveraged six times. Within five years, the stock price more than doubled, they paid off approximately $1 billion in debt and they are the lowest cost producer and are acquiring propane businesses in Canada and the United States. To achieve this turnaround, he removed 90 percent of the senior managers in three of the four core businesses—in a short period of time. Most CEOs state that it is a priority to surround oneself with the best people. Few act quickly enough. I asked him about his experience and his rapid approach.

It was fast, probably too fast. Well I don't think so. When you run a distribution business, leadership core competence is important. Not only were we in trouble financially (when I came in our debt was $60 million), but also we had problems in marketing, sales and technology. No one had digitalized the business or evaluated the talent. Every weekend [a regional manager and I] sat down for hours and reviewed products and went to branches and sat down with technicians and truck drivers in those branches to detect what was going on. I offered help. In one example, after three or four meetings and discussions with the President of X and his team, I took him aside and said, "You know this is not working out. It is not your fault. I can see that you do not have the right experience." He said, "Luc I get it. I understand what you are doing and how you are approaching it with all the businesses. I will be a good person. Help train me."

I responded, "No you had 12 months of training. There is more than one area [of deficiency] and it would take us three years to train you. We don't have the time." Within six months we had changed everybody. But it was a crisis.

Ideally, CEOs and executives retain independence in their decision making and judgment. This can be a lonely position, particularly when others are emotionally attached to a large initiative or a strategy that you determine you can no longer support. This was the case when Ed Clark decreed that TD would not offer mortgage-backed securities. Stakeholders benefit when executives stop activities or a popular project will not benefit the company or will no longer achieve the expected return on investment (ROI).

When providing advice to those who are destined for senior roles, it is worth expressing—it really is lonely at the top. Once you become CEO, why is it that your former peers can't drop by informally, with the Starbucks coffee like they always used to? Suddenly, informal access is now limited. There's a loneliness factor that organizations create for a variety of reasons. Of course, CEOs know that it is beneficial to surround themselves with people that are smarter than you and/or offer complementary skills. But it is true that when faced with a difficult situation or decision, the CEO has the ultimate accountability and the 'buck stops here.' That's when it can be lonely at the top.

—Sharon Ludlow

Brian MacNeill articulated that when he first became CEO he thought, "Oh my god, I'm going to make decisions now that are going to affect 10,000 people. Fortunately my advisors helped."

Sharon Ludlow describes a scenario in which she relied on the evidence to stop an initiative.

As we got further into it, I could sense that we were going to take the operations away from its core. When I reflected on all of the success that we had in the core business, and considered what was at risk, I said to those involved in the project, 'I absolutely don't think we should do this.' There was risk that it was going to divert the attention of people who had provided so much expertise and so much success in the core business. Chasing a shiny new object would have distracted us to the point where we might have impaired the core business. And so I stopped the initiative. I said, 'This has been interesting. I saw lots of creativity and a collaborative effort, but it isn't worth the risk.' I could also see that the team members were excited about the initiative but not seeing the risk to the core business. So I said, 'we're not going to proceed.' Not everyone agreed with that at the time.

After Sharon stopped the project, she observed the team members' thinking evolve. Many learned how to think strategically as a result of the decision.

What I observed was that for the project team, it was the proverbial forest and trees. Upon reflecting on the project, their thinking evolved to consider the bigger picture of how this might impact the existing organization. I saw individuals gain more respect than before for what we had already achieved. Their eyes were opened to the potential impact [of the initiative] to the organization. You could hear people say, "Ooh, I think I need to think more carefully and more strategically about how this might impact the company." I saw a little broader thinking, a little longer term thinking as opposed to a project oriented view.

Embrace Ambiguity or Seek Certainty at Your Potential Peril

Leading in ambiguous times requires flexibility and adaptability.

Consider the global shifts that have and will impose change on companies and citizens.

- Changing political agendas and priorities.
- The aging population and increasing life expectancy—putting increased pressure on healthcare, social services, and influencing immigration policies.
- Increased sentiment for nationalism as demonstrated by Brexit and Trump's campaign.
- Lower birthrates in many parts of North America and Europe.
- Debate over climate change and varied views on what actions should be taken.
- Ever-changing regulatory requirements.
- The priorities of millennials.
- Technological changes including the development of artificial intelligence, autonomous vehicles, robotics in manufacturing and medicine.

These and other trends require leaders to regularly consider the impacts on their business and the changing views of customers, employees, shareholders, regulators, and politicians. As a result, critical leadership capabilities include the ability to effectively operate within ambiguity by demonstrating flexibility and adaptability.

Exercise #2—Are you a navigator of change or a passenger?
360 degree CEOs are active listeners and consider multiple sources of information. They balance this with an inherent or learned ability and willingness to make adjustments as required. How do you know if you are demonstrating sufficient flexibility and adaptability in your personal and professional life?

Consider the questions below:

Can you identify two major changes that you initiated in your personal life over the past five years? This could include moving homes, changes to an important relationship, changing jobs within or outside of your organization, and so on.

- If you have initiated a significant change or changes in your personal life, you will have incurred the accompanying stress. Many years ago, people commonly referred to a scale that assigned scores to various life events and the higher the score, the greater the stress. The good news is that these life events and the accompanying stress generate new neural pathways and can boost your adaptability. Hopefully, you also developed some healthy strategies that you have applied or can apply to mitigate the stress of major change.

Have you made a geographic move of more than 120 miles?

- If so, how well did you adjust to new routines, developing new friendships and being away from long-time friends, family, and other support systems?
- Many people develop increased confidence and the ability to weather future imposed changes if they have moved or lived in multiple locations.
- It is important to note that multiple and frequent geographic moves generate a higher level of stress and can take the proverbial toll. If you have experienced this, ensure that you have sought out the support you may need to thrive in this situation.

Can you identify two to three change initiatives that you led at work in the past two to four years?

- 360 degree CEOs are not always change agents, but close to half of them are.
- Even when not active agents of change, these leaders take action when it is required, particularly when in the best interest of customers, employees, or shareholders. The choices may be challenging ones, but no leaders achieve this level of performance and the requisite reputation among their peers without having made changes when required. Often, these leaders initiated or supported organizational change throughout their career that may not have been in their immediate best interest. These leaders take a long view and have confidence that if they do the right things, in the end, it will all work out.
- Leaders who release hold on the status quo in spite of any fear of being unsuccessful or unpopular are demonstrating the required flexibility and develop the skills to adapt to all manners of change.

How do you react and respond when change is imposed upon you?

- Have you received feedback to indicate that others find you resistant to changing a course of action or, are you likely to respond, "If it's not broke, why fix it?" (American idiom)
- Many of us are more comfortable when we feel in control of our destiny and our situation and are therefore more comfortable with change that we initiate rather than change that has been imposed upon us.
- Some people make decisions quickly and with 80 percent of the facts. Others like to contemplate options for a longer period of time and/or ensure that all facts have been presented. There are benefits to both approaches. The key is being able to operate in both modes. When time allows,

take the time to consider data and evidence and the input of others whom you trust, but also have the ability to make decisions quickly when required, even if you do not yet have as much information as you would ideally like.

As you contemplate these questions, consider:

- Are you sufficiently extending your boundaries and pursuing new opportunities that may or may not meet your objectives?
- Are you feeling any discontent or a burr under your saddle to suggest that there is something that is no longer fulfilling you?
- Have you stayed in your current situation longer than you intended or out of a sense of responsibility or because it is easy and comfortable?
- When you initiated a change in the past, of job, residence, industry, adopted a new hobby, or traveled somewhere outside of your comfort zone, what benefits resulted that you had not anticipated?
- Think back to a time that a change was imposed on you that you were not happy about. How would you respond differently this time, if at all? What surprised you about the change?

CHAPTER 3

Celebrate Your Leadership Expression

Abandoning Celebrity Leadership

As with sports and movie actors, aspects of celebrity leadership have entered the boardroom. Cheryl Sandberg became a guide for the many women in business, who are still striving to do it all. Oprah has one of the most powerful brands on the planet. Jack Welch, Bill Clinton, and Donald Trump, while divergent in many ways, all leveraged larger-than-life personalities and extroversion to capture attention and acquire both followers and opposition. In some cases, opposition to their practices has contributed to their status as much as the adoration of loyal fans. When business leaders and CEOs attempt to model themselves after prominent personalities, it does not benefit them or the companies they work for. Celebrity leadership and the accompanying hero worship have created one-dimensional and stereotyped versions of the attributes of a successful CEO. Attempting to adopt others' behavior is like the ancient practice of binding women's feet. This squeezes your creativity and caps your potential.

Self-Awareness

As you will discover in the vignettes throughout this book, these leaders demonstrate self-awareness. This is consistent with what I have seen with my best clients and highly successful people. While they may have blind spots, when these gaps are identified, they give careful consideration to what they hear and they are willing to integrate that information into how they see themselves. They will often alter their conduct as a result. We will discuss methods for gathering feedback and increasing your levels of self-awareness.

Identifying Your Specific Leadership Strengths

After you have spent time donning another's wardrobe, it can take some time to strip away the layers and uncover your inherent gifts and the values that speak to you. Start the journey of discovery and unlock the doors blocking you from achieving your full potential.

How do you identify your best leadership attributes and tailor your own leadership beacon?

- ACT: Ask others. In what situations are you at your best? It can be very enlightening to seek information from a variety of sources. Consider asking people outside of the office, for example, colleagues who volunteer with you on a nonprofit board or in your role as coach of a children's sports team.

Growing as a Leader

You have clearly achieved a level of success to reach your current position. As I work with and interview 360 degree CEOs, no one is sitting on their laurels. Even if they have decided that they are in the final full-time role of their career, they are still striving to grow, improve, and expand—both personally and professionally.

- ACT: Participate in annual 360 degree reviews every one to two years. Do not rely simply on a survey and the results. Engage an objective third party to conduct the assessment and debrief you on the results. This can identify patterns of behavior and blind spots you may not have been aware of. This can be very beneficial, particularly if you create an action plan every year and implement it.
- ACT: Engage an executive coach or advisor. Just as elite athletes benefit from an experienced coach, so will you.

Surround yourself with peers who are striving to achieve what you are.

- ACT: Create or join informal or formal peer groups. Leadership is lonely and isolating at times. Many CEOs experience what I call the CEO island. CEOs who participate in peer groups are often surprised by how many of their issues and challenges are shared with others, crossing industries and geography. Trusted peers may challenge your assumptions or behavior in a way that your management team and perhaps even your board may not.

Exercise #3—Uncovering your capabilities

Reflect on your successes of both current and prior years. Many of us become unconsciously competent. What commonalities exist from your success? How did you untangle a particularly messy situation and achieve resolution for all stakeholders? What do you consistently receive positive feedback for?

Each year, evaluate yourself on the following:

- Business acumen
  - Are you a thought leader in your industry? Does the media seek you out? Are you asked to sit on panels at conferences? Do colleagues seek out your opinion? Do you have a breadth of expertise? Or are you highly skilled in a more singular way such as financial management, project management, marketing, or technology?
    - ACT: What is the one action you will take this year to promote your existing knowledge or to expand your business acumen?
- Decision making
  - Are you a rapid decision maker? Or do you prefer extensive analysis? Sometimes I observe newly appointed CEOs applying considerable rigor to a $75,000 decision or undertaking extensive due diligence when reviewing vendor proposals. In many of these cases, they have not adjusted their practices to align with their new level of responsibility.
    - ACT: Consider the ROI for two recent decisions. Are you making decisions that could or should be made by one of your direct reports? Are you applying

a balanced level of rigor before taking action? Or are
you leaping and then having to course correct later?

- Judgment
  - o Good judgment is a critical attribute to maintaining
    your reputation, managing organizational risk, respond-
    ing to unexpected and difficult client or employee situa-
    tions, and weathering challenging economic or political
    environments.
    - ACT: What feedback have you received from your
      board or direct reports regarding your judgment?
      When you reflect on the past several months, were
      there any situations in which you did not heed your
      inner voice or your instincts? If so, did this resolve in
      a better or worse outcome than you expected? If your
      judgment is consistently sound, what can you do to
      further develop the judgment of those who report
      to you?

- Emotional strength
  - o How well are you managing strong emotions? Do you
    hold your anger or excitement at bay? Or do you openly
    share what you are feeling? Do you modify how you
    react based on the audience? Are you seen as a calm,
    constant, and predictable leader who does not hold
    back from displaying emotion and does so in a way that
    creates an open and healthy environment?
    - ACT: Do you lose sleep when encountering negative
      emotions including anger, frustration, impatience,
      and so on? Are you readily displaying your frustration
      to your management team? If so, are you doing so to
      a healthy degree? Or is it causing people to hold back
      from giving you honest feedback or bad news for fear
      of your reaction? Are you supressing your emotions
      to such an extent that your management team does
      not recognize your dissatisfaction and anger? Is this
      an area in which you would benefit from acquiring

new skills in handling conflict? Perhaps you have
developed healthy outlets for emotions. These often
include talking it through with a supportive spouse,
exercise, keeping a journal, and so on. If this is the
case, is there someone on your team who would
benefit from understanding your coping mechanisms?

Communicating with Power

Frank Reynolds* was President and CEO of a $3 billion bank in
the United States. A few years ago, his bank had to repay customers
approximately $1.5 million in overcharged fees. When the issue was
uncovered, Frank learned that one of his executives had been aware of
the overcharging for a few years and determined it immaterial. Frank
did not agree. Neither would the public nor the regulators.

Once the incident was resolved, we discussed strategies for
preventing similar situations in future. Frank was understandably
angry and disappointed that this information had been kept from him.
What surprised me was that he withheld his frustration from his management team overall. He very purposefully donned not just a calm
but almost laissez-faire manner when addressing the mis-judgment
with his team. His intentions were good—he did not want to intim-
idate anyone or shoot the messenger. He also felt some responsibility
for the situation, but his filtered response exacerbated the problem. In
spite of a lawsuit and a senior-level termination, his team was inadver-
tently interpreting his behavior as "people will make mistakes; I cannot
be responsible for what they do." Once he realized this, we crafted a
dialogue that empowered his leaders and also defined clear accountability for decision making in future. He quickly learned how to lead
even more effectively and his executive team is more skilled in decision
making, mitigating risk for the bank.

*name changed

CHAPTER 4

Failure is Foundational to Innovation

Failure helps you learn very quickly. It is part of the necessary ingredient for growing quickly and transforming. Failure has got a bad rap and we [society and leaders] avoid it like the plague. That means we avoid being spectacular as well.

—Suzanne West

Failing Up

When I first met Jennifer*, she was the CEO of a $1 billion oil and gas company. She carried the reputation of being smart, strategic, and decisive. I learned that she was also an executive who supported learning through mistakes.

Two years before, her CFO had independently made the decision to invest a considerable amount of their cash holdings in AAA-rated securities. Unfortunately, due to unforeseen issues with the issuer of the securities, Jennifer's company had lost a material amount of money on the investment. The board was naturally upset and called for the resignation of the CFO. After careful consideration, Jennifer disagreed. While the CFO had not sought approval for the securities purchase, he had acted within accordance to the corporate policies. Secondly, his judgment was sound. Had the policy required him to seek approval of the board and/or CEO, all would have supported the investment. In a low interest rate environment, they wanted a reasonable rate of return on their cash holdings and the securities were highly rated.

In fact, Jennifer relayed to me, the CFO was expecting to be asked to resign. By the board and CEO supporting him, he would be particularly prudent in mitigating risk in future and would be fiercely loyal to the company. Jennifer also acknowledged her accountability in having policies that allowed for independent decisions of such a significant nature. The board accepted Jennifer's argument and accompanying rationale. Jennifer was proud of her decision and the outcome and grateful for the ultimate support of the board.

* name changed

Fear of failure is ingrained in us from an early age. Historically, we were awarded largely for achievement—good grades in school, strong performance on sports teams and high SAT scores. This transitioned seamlessly into adulthood where, within our workplaces, we are recognized for meeting or exceeding sales targets, expense reduction, completion of projects on time and on budget, achieving ROI on mergers and acquisitions, strong earnings per share (EPS), and quarter over quarter improved financial performance.

In recent decades in North America, recognition of school age children has evolved to include certificates and awards for participation and/or recognition simply for showing up. This has evolved in part due to a growing resistance to differentiation and perceived competition. This has not reduced our fear of failure. If anything, it ill-prepares students for the workplace and can stifle innovation.

There are benefits in overcoming our fear of failure. We may become more comfortable with taking calculated risk. We can develop methods for testing ideas and concepts that allow us to more effectively evaluate options. We may generate breakthrough ideas.

When I [joined Enmax] someone said to me, "Look, you can't fall off the floor. When you know things are bad and you have a turnaround situation, you probably have only one way to go so don't focus on failure." It is helpful to have people remind you of those things every now and then.

—Gianna Manes

Failure is the foundation to innovation. When we play safe, we cannot conceive the disruptors that may change our industry or our organization.

While enabling failure in a purposeful way will foster innovation, it is also important to understand the nature of your particular organization and industry. Cal Yonker and I discussed this.

> What is the definition of innovation?... It is the creation of something new. I think the CEO needs to understand if their business is set up to be revolutionary or evolutionary, as there are a lot of implications in the answer, including your financial model. The organization that I run is evolutionary, not revolutionary. There are folks out there who are revolutionizing big businesses and that are spending hundreds of millions of dollars revolutionizing or start ups that are heavily funded to do those things. Our game is evolutionary. It's making sure that we are making solid incremental changes to the way we do business to provide better value to our customer. The role of CEO of this company is about understanding "where are the areas that we do need to evolve and become better?" Also, understanding how that drives value to our customers and how that differentiates what we do from our competitors. That's the general role innovation plays in our company.

Fortunately more and more executives understand the learning and innovation that can result from failed ventures and mistakes, when leaders understand how to best respond and foster a learning environment. Colleen Abdoulah demonstrated this in a way that few CEOs have. This was one contributor to the success of WOW, a company that grew from ~$200 million in revenue to $1.1 billion in revenue, and from 600 to 3,200 employees in a relatively short period of time.

> We created a Courage Award because, saying, "hey, make mistakes, that's how we all learn," nobody believed me. Everyone would say, "She doesn't mean that. The first big mistake we make, I'm going to get axed." That was everybody's experience. I wanted to create the award specifically to prove that I meant it.

I remember that first awardee of the Courage Award; he was 58. He was the head of our field operations. The details don't matter but when our group came into his [region], he knew they weren't ready. He knew that the infrastructure wasn't where it needed to be, that they needed about three more months. But he also knew that we were on a tight timeline and if we met the timeline, we would save about a million and a half dollars. So he didn't say anything, it didn't go well, it shut things down and we had customer impact. It was just a mess for a good week or two. When we conducted our post-mortem, we asked, "What happened? How did this happen? You said it was OK." He said, "I know. I said it was OK because I was worried about staying on schedule. I was worried about looking like a failure. I wanted my team to be the ones that kept us on track. And I was scared to say otherwise."

So we gave him the award. It was a three-day trip for him and his wife. At the dinner where we were presenting the awards, he got up and he held his award, and he said, "I'm an old dog and I've been in this business for almost 30 years and I've been told when mistakes happen we should learn from them. I never believed it until now. I made a big mistake that cost us a lot of time and money and I'm here enjoying an all-expense paid trip with my wife. I've never even travelled outside of Michigan; we've not been on a plane before. This is awesome. I have learned something that I will take to my grave."

From that point on when people made mistakes it was not an embarrassment to win that award because we learned from it. People really started to embrace that. It was a learning environment. Every mistake made us better. We did our post-mortems. We talked about [the situation] without blame, without anybody getting fired and we just moved on to the next project.

Colleen elaborated with an important point. When you are seeking to create a culture of accountability, of innovation and supporting continuous learning, you have to operationalize the desired culture.

Trust is low in business. Leadership is low, because things are said but not done. If you don't develop trust early on in your organization, you're not going to get the kind of creativity and innovation and risk taking that you need to be smart and smarter than your competitors and faster. Our competitive motto was "Learn faster, execute better." [We asked ourselves] "are we learning faster than they are? And then from that learning, can we execute better?"

Exercise #4—Failing Up

What are the unrealized opportunities in your company or on your team? How do you foster an environment in which people can fail up?

- Share your failure stories.
  - Identify some examples from your own experience—personal or professional.
  - Share them at town hall meetings, in your video updates, or when meeting with your teams.
  - Share what you learned from the experience and how you or others benefitted.
- Be a visible and vocal supporter for large change efforts, such as an acquisition, new ERP system, new product or service offering, and so on.
  - The employees involved in these change initiatives are typically facing two opposing forces: resistance from peers, colleagues, and perhaps customers, and an expectation that the project is successful.
  - By nature, these changes are highly visible and the implementation is under scrutiny by many, including their immediate bosses and potentially you, the board, and others.
  - The resistors may sometimes gleefully hold up these failures as evidence to support their own resistance.
  - Speak about the value of failure and mistakes as fodder for innovation.

- Define parameters.
  - Beyond signing authority for expenses, what are the boundaries within which you are comfortable tolerating failure? Your own risk tolerance has a bearing here.
  - You may have a high tolerance for risk overall. This is particularly true of entrepreneurs. However, your tolerance will vary depending on the category and needs to be clearly specified.
  - You will likely have zero tolerance for mistakes that affect health and safety, for harassment or fraud, and so on.
  - If you tend to be risk-averse overall, to foster innovation you may need to demonstrate greater latitude. Ask trusted members of your team for their feedback in this area.
  - Can you create specific parameters?
    - One of my retail clients empowered customer facing and frontline employees to "spend" up to $25 to resolve a customer issue or mistake, regardless of who made the error.
    - Another client regularly allows a 7 percent contingency on large projects to fund "testing of unique and previously unidentified concepts that may fail."
- Recognize failures as learning opportunities.
  - The purpose is not to create a free-for-all environment of anything goes, but rather to demonstrate that failure can contribute to innovation and better outcomes.
  - Be selective and recognize the failures that resulted from appropriate trial and error and from sound judgment.

Innovation is not only creating new products and services but innovation can also be an approach to complex situations, and I think about my history and the teams that I worked with. We were drawn to complexity. We have that here at Hydro One today and it's how we create a competitive advantage by demonstrating the ability to overcome that complexity or solve it. To come out the other side, that puts us in a leadership position.

When I think about Viterra, we did that over and over and over which is why we became so strong in the field and ultimately why so many companies came in to buy Viterra all at the same time, creating a very unique and high-profile auction of peers, large peers that wanted to buy because we had created a business born out of complexity and made simple. And executed. And that complexity had to be demonstrated and it takes a leader to be able to say, "I remember the former CFO from another company said we can't because of these reasons, but we need to be able to turn and say it's not only going to be that hard but twice as hard as that and that is exactly what we are going to do." Showing leadership in the face of naysayers or someone who believes it can't be done, I really enjoy working with teams that enjoy complexity because I believe that in complexity lies opportunity.

—Mayo Schmidt

CHAPTER 5

The CEO and Board Relationship

Whether in a private or public company, the CEO's relationship with the board can be one of the most important relationships and has the potential to be precarious or career enhancing and rewarding. The role of the board is to set the strategy for the company. The role of the CEO and his or her management team is to execute on that strategy. When boards operate effectively, they provide governance and oversight and do not dictate how management should run the company. Boards of large, publicly run companies are typically high functioning. The directors have a wealth of executive experience, typically with considerable director experience and formal board education.

In small, private, or family-run enterprises, directors may not have as much experience and may cross from governance to operations on occasion. As well, for family-run businesses it can be difficult to separate relationships and family loyalties from what is in the best interest of the company, particularly when faced with difficult decisions. This can be more difficult for the CEO and the management team than a more unbiased board.

As a director, you can have considerable influence. Encourage your director colleagues to participate in director education and/or propose recruiting more experienced directors. If you are a CEO in this situation, address the situation respectfully with the board chair or the chair of the governance and nominating committee. Provide evidence of the impacts resulting from the board stepping into operations or family dynamics. In most cases, directors will be receptive to feedback if approached in a constructive and collaborative manner.

CEO in the Driver's Seat

The relationship with your board is largely influenced by how you conduct yourself. This commences before you accept the top job and of course extends through the life of your joint relationship and changes in board complement.

A very savvy and self-aware CEO recanted this story:

We [she and the board] had very good discussions. I was interested in the role, I had decades of experience in the industry and while I could see the board was quite keen, I also sensed reticence with some of the directors and I was not sure why. I realized that my style, my gender and my physical appearance were different than my predecessor and different than what some of them envisioned as a powerful CEO in the industry. I knew I was highly qualified to do the job, but there was nothing I could do to change who I was.

She had an honest conversation with some of the directors and said:

If you want a 50+ year old male, former college athlete who stands 6 feet tall and whose voice commands a room, that is not me. I will never be that person. I know this industry very well and I know how to effectively lead this company into the future. But if you believe you need what I described then you need to go and find someone else.

This was a carefully considered approach on her part. It may have resulted in her not being offered the position but if she did not fit what they believed they required, it would not have been the best fit for the CEO, the board, or the company. She held this conversation only after she had established as much trust and mutual respect as was possible within the somewhat limited duration of a CEO selection. She held this conversation in a highly respectful and non-challenging manner. If some of the directors did hold such a bias, it may have been unconscious on their part as such perceptions often are. This CEO's approach in this situation increased the likelihood of successfully navigating difficult decisions in the future by being forthright in her approach.

In this example, the CEO displayed attributes that are highly correlated to successful leaders: intuition, self-awareness, self-confidence, humility, and assertiveness. She also understood the nature of the relationships between board and CEO.

The information in the following sections is applicable to CEOs and boards for companies of all sizes and for publicly or privately held and not for profit.

Neither Friends Nor Confidantes

CEO and director relationships are unique from other relationships. The directors are not friends, nor are they confidantes. In some situations, they may end up acting in one of these ways but that is not always the case. Directors must hold CEOs personally accountable for the success of the company. Some new CEOs are surprised to discover that while they think they now have carte blanche to run the company, sometimes years after vying for the role, they now have 10 to 12 bosses.

Navigate the White Water

Years ago a wise mentor advised me to consider directors as the white water in a class 4 rapids. Part of my responsibility was to anticipate and prepare for the white water, not wait until I was in the swirl before reacting. Wise CEOs take the lead when investing in director knowledge and relationships.

- Anticipate what information the directors will be seeking and what questions they are likely to ask. This should become easier over time as you work with them.
- Hold one-on-one meetings.
- Ask directors what corporate performance is most important and on what they are seeking regular updates. Expect this to

change over time. Topics could include the status of: a new point of sale system that is visible to customers, a new product or service offering, trend of whistleblower reporting, revenue, expense reduction initiatives, and so on.

- Provide e-mail updates on a regular and consistent basis on the one or two priority items.

- Don't attend board meetings thinking you need to demonstrate that you are one of the smartest people in the room, or even worse, thinking you are the smartest person in the room.
  - Directors would rather participate in a discussion and debate, drawing on their experiences and judgment rather than sitting through the proverbial dog and pony show with numerous slides and reporting from management.
  - Don't mistake this for thinking you do not need to provide reporting, data, and trend analysis. You most certainly do, see the previous point on e-mail updates. But balance information sharing with discussion. Ask your directors how much information they want and for what purposes.

- Seek feedback and guidance from directors outside of and in advance of board meetings. Ideally, let your board chair know that you are doing this and use the discussions primarily to seek guidance on strategy.

- Use the informal meetings to discover where directors may have disagreement or apprehension so that you can be well prepared for the discussion at the board table.

- The board's primary responsibility is CEO succession. To that end, ensure that the members of your management team engage with the board with some frequency. These interactions will develop management's communication skills and further their confidence in dealing with directors. Some of the directors may provide excellent guidance to managers, usually drawing on their areas of expertise such as technology, marketing, finance, M&A, and so on.
  - A few years ago, a CEO required an unexpected medical leave. The COO stepped in to act as interim CEO for several weeks. Because the board had prior exposure to

the COO, there was greater confidence that the company would operate effectively and the directors were familiar with the COO's expertise and areas in which he lacked experience.

- Like CEOs, directors are accustomed to wielding influence and have confidence in their own knowledge and judgment. The wise CEO demonstrates openness to challenges, is prepared to consider another point of view, and is careful to not appear defensive. This contributes to stronger CEO/board relationships and increases the likelihood that you will retain your role for a period of time.

It is helpful to understand the attributes and responsibilities of an effective board chair and the directors. Russell Reynolds Associates are an authority in this area and some of the following information has been drawn from their files.

www.russellreynolds.com

The Chair's Role in Fostering a Relationship with the CEO

The chair is the most important member of the board. An effective chair will oversee governance practices, will advocate for the CEO, and will hold the difficult conversations that may be required with the CEO or directors. The fortunate CEO has a chair that effectively advises the CEO and serves as an important mentor and advisor.

As a board chair, Randy Findlay seeks to participate with his CEO in a collaborative and supportive manner, "I don't know if [the chair role is] a mentor to the CEO, but it is important to be a sounding board for the CEO." In Randy's experience, the CEO should be able to have some really good conversations about personal things, including how to best manage one's life or similar topics.

[Over a breakfast] meeting I said to the CEO, "influencing the board on this important decision is our job." We were looking at something new and the board didn't fully understand it and [the CEO really wanted] do it. In that case, he and I have to figure out how to do it. We have to slow down or we have to catch everyone up. It is about understanding the interaction between board and management. Interaction on our board is great. We have diverse people with diverse backgrounds. We need to remember that not only are their backgrounds different but also their thought processes, and how they get to an answer, how they gather what they need [to make a decision]. [The chair needs to ensure] we are not working at the slowest speed and also not working at the fastest speed and pushing people who are a little bit thoughtful and want to take some time. Also you have to try to hold back the person that says "let's just get on with it."

Other responsibilities of the board chair are as follows:

- Available and accessible to the CEO to advise on strategic decisions and how to appropriately execute on the approved strategy.
- Asks great questions. An effective chair (or director) will ask thoughtful, thought-provoking questions about strategy and organizational performance.
- Is decisive and action-oriented, particularly to ensure that the board is meeting the standards of governance and its fiduciary responsibilities. Will step in without hesitation and lend support in a crisis situation.
- Actively participates in strategy and succession. The best board chair leads board approval of strategy but does not overstep and attempt to develop the strategy. Good chairs demonstrate ownership of CEO succession.
- As noted earlier in this chapter, director roles are time consuming and this is particularly true for the chair. A board chair is expected to demonstrate his or her full commitment and to be highly engaged. The chair sets the tone for all directors through his or her active commitment at meetings, in all discussions, and so on.
- The chair collaborates with the CEO to establish expectations and set agendas, rules of engagement, and decision-making processes.

- The chair shows the way in building professional relationships with key members of the management team. He or she understands the responsibilities, the areas of expertise, the personalities, and the career ambitions of each of these individuals.

Responsibilities of Directors

- Directors are expected to advise on strategic decisions and provide thoughtful, actionable guidance on implementing the strategy. Like the chair, the best directors are accessible to the CEO as required.
- Capable directors ask probing, penetrating questions and do not shy away from asking tough questions of the CEO or their peers. They demonstrate leadership courage, just as identified for the 360 degree CEO.
- Directors act decisively and will step in to assist during a crisis or situations in which more effort is required. The best directors maintain a deep commitment to the performance of the organization, and this commitment clearly is reflected in their level of engagement on issues of critical importance to the performance of the company.

How you engage with your board has considerable bearing on the relationship. Let's consider two examples.

In the first example, the CEO was running a $400M not-for-profit company. When the CEO joined the company, it was his first time in a CEO role and his first foray into the not-for-profit sector. Within 90 days, he discovered more issues than he had anticipated. During the first year, the company was caught up in a public debacle that they had not caused. Today, the CEO has high praise for the board chair and their support and wisdom during the first 18 months. Five years later, company results are stellar. The organization has grown, community support is high, and the board recently approved a dynamic new growth strategy.

What factors contributed to this success story? CEO humility, a skilled board chair, and shared commitment to the company's success.

CEO Humility

Sometimes CEOs are reluctant to display vulnerability for fear that the board will think they are "not up for the job." This is flawed thinking. With rare exception, board chairs have experienced their own share of successes and failures and can be an excellent source of advice and counsel. In this particular case, the CEO proactively sought advice of the chair when responding to sensitive issues. Many times this took the form of a 15-minute conference call. In my experience as a board chair and also in my work with clients, highly successful CEOs utilize this strategy. A brief phone call in advance of taking action mitigates risk and increases the likelihood of achieving the desired results. Why is this? The discussion may identify a blind spot in thinking or provide an alternative path and allows the senior leader to think aloud and test their approach and actions before proceeding. It can also heighten the leader's confidence and readiness; this benefits everyone.

> You asked about humility and I think about receiving accolades for things and what it feels like being humble. You mentioned Ed Clark so maybe that's why this comes to mind. I came into Viterra at a time when they were in a financial crisis. That was the start of my leadership, starting at the bottom and we worked through all of that in really, really hard, difficult times. People would think it was easier to leave the organization than to stay because of the heavy lifting we had to do. At the end of all that, a man named Ed Clark came to me and said he respected us for the things that the teams had done which was everything that they said they were going to do through some perilous days, weeks and years and that his bank was willing to support the company by allowing us a significant line of credit to go and do the ambitious things that we had in our minds and plans. That was the launch of the growth of Viterra from

a regional company to a global powerhouse and Ed Clark was a catalyst because he believed in us. He had a bird's eye view of the restructuring and recognized the things we were doing. He gave us the capital to [proceed with] the unique things we did. It was a courageous choice on his part. In my career, one of the greatest compliments was his support after watching the organization work through a lot of tough stuff.

—Mayo Schmidt

While Mayo was responding to my question about humility, he highlighted many of the traits that contributed to Ed Clark being a historic leader—his vision, his willingness to take calculated risk, and his humility.

Sharon Ludlow spoke about being vulnerable at the board table and with her executives.

You need to show vulnerability. Having other team members around you with a complementary skill set is important. When we were embarking on something new, I would turn to one or two of my key people and say, 'I have elements of how I think we can approach this initiative but I need you to be there with me, either in support of or with technical aspects or to help lead a piece of it.'

You don't want to go into a board meeting alone and say 'well I can't answer that question, I need my team to answer all questions.' Instead, you go to the table and present it as, 'here is the initiative and our path forward. I'm presenting on behalf of the organization and acknowledge all of the team members that were involved.' Most of the time those involved will be in the room for the discussion and would be able to respond and/ or lead portions of the presentation if you wanted to exhibit their leadership capabilities.

It gives the directors visibility to the talent and teamwork in the organization, but it also demonstrates the vulnerability of the CEO as the directors realize that CEOs cannot accomplish it all alone. In my case, the directors view this as 'Sharon is coming to the table with a well-considered plan and leveraged all the expertise of her team.'

Addressing vulnerability is demonstrated by drawing on others' expertise and by admitting, 'I don't know everything and therefore I need you just as much as you need me. If you're supporting me, I'm supporting you. Together we'll have a much better solution.' And our stakeholders, in this case the board, will see that and we'll have a better solution for everyone all around.

Also, because they were involved, the team wholly supported the initiative because they felt they were engaged and empowered at a very senior level. They also respected the fact that it was my role to present to the board and to be accountable to the board if something went wrong. They felt proud to be part of it. In other organizations I have seen examples of situations where people were asked to be part of a project team, contributed ideas and then felt that they weren't given appropriate credit.

Skilled Board Chair

Several trends are contributing to more effective boards. Fortunately, albeit slowly, there is a positive trend of increased board diversity—on public boards in particular. Term limits are more common as are restrictions on the number of boards one can participate on. For decades, well-connected individuals could participate as active directors on 10+ corporate boards for Fortune 500 companies. A small number of individuals wielded a great deal of influence and interacted, sometimes, in an almost incestuous manner. Greater regulation, shareholder activism, increased director liability, and baby boomers seeking board positions have all led to the creation and growth of director and board education. The ICD in Canada, National Association of Board Directors in the United States, and IOD in the United Kingdom are leading the way in providing director education.

Board chairs are now most often highly skilled—particularly in publicly held companies. They are becoming more versed in the difference between governance and operations. When they are elected positions and where term limits exist, chairs typically hold considerable experience in leadership, business acumen, stakeholder engagement, risk management, and governance.

In the example we are appraising, the board chairs were highly skilled business leaders, running companies of significant scale. When the CEO engaged their assistance in problem solving and risk mitigation, they provided sound advice. In addition, and this is important, because the CEO engaged them before taking action in high-risk situations, there was shared ownership. If the results and outcomes were not as expected, the CEO was not considered wholly responsible and the chairs would counter any negative feedback from the other directors and/or politicians or members of the community. CEOs shoulder a great deal of responsibility and sometimes forget that they do not have to fly solo!

Shared Commitment to the Company's Success

Gone are the days when directors could dedicate somewhat minimal time to their board responsibilities. In the 1970s and 1980s, many of North America's elite establishment sat on multiple boards simultaneously. They comprised a relatively small, well-connected group, typically white males from Ivy League schools with solid business acumen and, often, military experience. This is no longer possible. Participating as a director on three to four public, private, or crown corporation boards is the most that is manageable. Director roles are more demanding and time consuming; this is particularly true for committee and board chairs. The increased workload, responsibility, and liability have weeded out those who are not fully committed to the organization they are representing. While there are some exceptions, directors today are committed to the success of the organization and the CEO. The best board chairs are keen to offer wisdom, insight, and to act as a mentor and sounding board for the CEO.

In the example described here, the board chair acted as an ambassador for the organization, visibly and vocally demonstrating their support to the community, in the board room, with management and staff, and when engaging one-on-one meeting with the CEO. This support alleviated the CEO isolation that I so often observe and mitigated risk to all stakeholders.

In the second example, the CEO was running a $5B logistics company. After four years in her role, she loved her job. With the support of the board, she opportunistically and proactively created a stellar executive leadership team. When the Senior Vice President of Corporate Services retired, the CEO selected a replacement from another part of the country with deep retail experience in the consumer goods industry. When the CEO determined that her CFO was not operating at a strategic level, she replaced him with a highly experienced strategic thinker with potential to succeed her as CEO.

The CEO relished the industry, the customers, the commercial aspects of the business, and the large metropolitan center she had relocated to four years earlier. However, there was one rather large fly in the ointment—she had a poor relationship with several of the directors, and it showed. Some of her frustration with the board was justified. The board bylaws did not include term limits or attendance requirements for board meetings. Most of the board members were from the same state and hailed from the transportation industry. While all were highly capable individuals, the lack of diversity sometimes contributed to groupthink and attachment to the status quo. In addition, surprisingly few of the board members had completed director education, nor had they participated as a group in any professional development.

There is an old adage that one can be "dead right." In her frustration, the CEO aligned herself with the SVP of Corporate Services and actively spoke critically about the board's effectiveness. While she maintained a good relationship with the vice chair, her frequent criticism alienated the board chair. Here is what the board saw: an arrogant CEO who undervalued the collective wisdom of the directors; a CEO negatively influencing the opinions and therefore, judgment, of at least one of the executive leadership team; and a CEO who "forgot" who hired her and assessed her performance and was acting in a disrespectful manner. The board was also uncomfortable with the fact that the CEO was aligning herself with one of the executives rather than with the vice chair (who was a supporter) and/or other directors. They viewed this as immature executive behavior.

Corporate performance reached new heights. EBITA exceeded objectives for three years. Customers were satisfied, safety audits were clean, and employee engagement was at historically high levels. However, the board and CEO relationship continued to deteriorate. Perhaps illogically but certainly consistent with human behavior, as the CEO continued to criticize, director behavior became more entrenched. In counseling the CEO, I advised her to seek a position with another company and to advise the board of her intent so that they could work together on a mutually beneficial and agreed-to transition. That is what she did. She had an honest conversation with the board chair and vice chair. They agreed to engage in confidential CEO recruitment with a recruiter. They would support the CEO in conducting a quiet job search so long as she remained with the organization for at least six months. Together, they created the communications plan and in the end, the CEO actively participated in selecting her successor. Herein lies the irony... with external advice and assistance, the CEO and board worked together more effectively than they had for the prior 48 months. The public and internal announcements were well managed and the market viewed the leadership change in a favorable manner. Shortly after the CEO departure, the board updated their bylaws to include annual board effectiveness evaluation, term limits, diversity targets, and minimum requirements for meeting attendance among other changes. They also engaged in professional development activities with the new CEO.

What characterized the different outcome in the second example? Could this talented and previouslyx, highly successful CEO have influenced the desired changes and recovered her relationship with the board? Unlikely. She may have been able to affect these positive changes earlier *had she demonstrated greater humility*. There was shared commitment to the company's success but the CEO did not demonstrate sufficient humility and the directors lacked some of the essential skills.

CHAPTER 6

Mindful of the Full Spectrum of Stakeholders

Operating in the 360 Degree Business Environment

Global access to the Internet and the development of social media has forever changed your businesses and how you influence your customers, colleagues, and employees. The more senior one's position in the organizational hierarchy, the less likely you may be to hear challenging and potentially useful feedback. If you are leading a large organization, you may also be sheltered from some decisions being made within the organization and, therefore, unaware of some of the potential risks. You know that ignorance rarely provides bliss and that is certainly true when it comes to feedback and being aware of potentially bad news. Let's consider some examples.

In 2016, TD Canada Trust, the Canadian retail-banking arm of TD Bank Financial Group, had won the JD Power Award for highest in customer satisfaction (among big five banks) for 10 consecutive years. In early 2017, their retail banking operation again made news but this time for a different reason. Employees interviewed by CBC Radio said they experienced "incredible pressure" to meet "unrealistic" sales targets resulting in them signing up customers for unnecessary financial products. Other former and then-current TD employees suggested that they felt it necessary to break the law to meet sales targets and to retain employment. They spoke of a stressful work environment and psychological problems such as anxiety and depression.

In these situations, impact can be swift and severe. Within days of the first news story, TD shares took a negative hit of 5.5 percent, suffering their worst single day since the global financial crisis eight years earlier and eliminating all gains made that year. Rapidly, Rosen Law Firm announced that they were preparing a class-action lawsuit on behalf of TD Bank investors.

This debacle followed on the heels of Wells Fargo's fines of US$185 million and the termination of thousands of employees after it was revealed that the bank created millions of fake bank accounts. One would expect that TD and other well-respected and well-run financial institutions would have imposed greater diligence following Wells Fargo. Perhaps they did or they may have felt secure due to their track record of customer satisfaction and what they stated in their press release: TD Bank has "procedures in place designed to monitor sales practices and to detect issues should they arise," including a system for tracking customer complaints. "For the 12-month period ended January 31, 2017, of the many interactions with our millions of Canadian personal banking customers, we received only a few hundred such complaints related to sales practices compliance. These were investigated and handled in accordance with our procedures," said the press release.

http://cbc.ca/news/business/td-bank-defensive-1.4022394

Variables that Impact Severity

The impacts of these situations can vary and are dependent on your prior reputation and how your company spokesperson and most senior leadership respond to the crisis situation. When you have amassed a substantive amount of collateral through trust built with your shareholders, your customers, and your communities, your reputation may be better able to withstand the storm. If you have not built the goodwill over time, or if the response to the public is not carefully considered, you are at risk of such situations that have a larger impact. Let's compare a few examples that all occurred within a month of each other.

It is oft said that reputation takes years to build and only a moment to destroy. In the case of Bill O'Reilly, US political commentator removed from his position at Fox TV in spring 2017, this was definitely the case. His alleged actions were so widespread and reprehensible that his personal and professional reputation took an irreversible hit.

In contrast, at the time of the TD debacle, analysts expressed little concern and indicated that while the situation would naturally be compared to Wells Fargo, the collateral damage was unlikely to be of equal proportions. This calm response resulted from TD's solid reputation in the marketplace, built over many years and demonstrated by 10 years of recognition for customer satisfaction. In addition, the leadership team was regarded as highly ethical and as demonstrating strong judgment.

This collateral with your stakeholders takes years to build. The Canadian banks fared well during the global economic crisis in comparison to US banks. Among this esteemed group, TD stood out as a leader as they had not invested in mortgage-backed securities. So it is with your company and your role within it. If you consistently do the right thing, making decisions that are ethical and moral, which would make your mother proud, you will build the trust of those around you. How you handle these situations is keenly important for your own reputation as well as that of the company or division. Bharat Masrani, CEO of TD Bank made public statements on Friday and Sunday evenings of the week the news broke and the bank stocks took a hit.

TD has "a long history of providing great customer service. TD is in the trust business. We know we must earn our customers' trust before we earn their business. Everything we do is about earning and sustaining the trust of those we serve."

In contrast, after United Airlines customers posted video of a gentleman being bodily removed from a flight, it was two days before the CEO Oscar Munoz apologized. To make it worse, he first publicly cast blame on the customer and airport security and it was reported that he first praised employees in an internal memo before issuing an apology to the customer, Dr. Dao. The global community judged his behavior as avoiding responsibility rather than leveraging his authority and position to demonstrate personal responsibility and accountability. United Airlines employs over 100,000 people. When this public relations nightmare hit the press, Munoz could have modeled integrity, respect, and accountability, positively reinforcing values of the organization. The airline executive could have then used this to reinforce expected behavior of all employees to customers and to each other. Consider the massive impact this could have had on an organization for years to come. Instead, it cost the airline considerably in loss of share price, revenues, reputation, and employee engagement.

In summary, our lessons for this 24/7 world of transparency are these:

- It is as worthwhile as ever to construct and maintain your reputation and, in particular, your attributes of integrity, reliability, and compassion.
  - Every day, in each interaction with your customers, clients, shareholders, employees, prospects, and members of the community, you have an opportunity to create a lasting affirmative reputation. This contributes to your personal brand and your company brand.
  - When you demonstrate consistent, ethical and moral decisions and actions over the long term, you may be able to more quickly recover from negative publicity or mistakes.
  - One of my CEO clients and I shared our views on the changing political environment, the resurgence in nationalist sentiment across the globe and the impacts on economies and regular citizens. We agreed that while we naturally had sometimes strong positive or negative views, we refrained from sharing these in any public way, recognizing that our views would reflect on and could be seen as representing the views of the companies we run, not just our own personal opinions. For that reason, we are selective in what we say and the forums in which we say it.
- Respond rapidly and carefully when warranted.
  - Bharat Masrani publicly responded within a few days and shouldered responsibility. Oscar Munoz commented quickly but to apportion blame. You will not always have all required information and until you do, acknowledge your awareness of the situation and take responsibility as is appropriate.
- Not everyone will be nice. Not all news will be accurate. It is not fair. It is not right. Get over it.
  - At one time we trusted our media icons, individuals such as Walter Cronkite and Peter Mansbridge. Today anyone can behave as a quasi-journalist or reporter, sharing the equivalent of a news feed from their smart phone onboard an

airplane flight, at a political rally, in a war zone, or as law enforcement respond to a crisis.

o It is natural to respond defensively and with hurt or anger when an opponent or competitor speaks out against our organization or us. We cannot control others' actions but we can apply what we have learned in other parts of our lives—managing how we respond to the situation.

o When responding to negative feedback or to a crisis situation, utilize your in-house media relations' people or seek outside expertise. Carefully crafted communication will be highly beneficial.

o Do not use your personal social media accounts or your considerable influence to respond or comment. Silence may be criticized but it cannot be quoted!

Lessons from GMO

Seedless green grapes—an innocuous staple in many grocery stores, they receive little attention. With over a dozen varieties, this product has been available to us for decades, a fraction of the estimated 6,000 to 8,000 years that man has been eating grapes. If one considered the widespread popularity of seedless grapes, accounting for 70 percent of the world's grape consumption, would food producers have anticipated highly attended protests in China for genetically modified oatmeal, consumer fear over new varieties of tomatoes, and so on? Many factors have fueled the growth in genetically modified foods—population growth, climate—droughts or heavy rains and accompanying melds, consumer demand for fresh produce at all times of the year and from well outside a 100 mile radius of their homes and farmers seeking higher yields and improved financial health.

What is the GMO equivalent for your business? Consumers are less trusting of big business and leaders of these organizations than they are of strangers. When surveyed, respondents in most western countries express an overall higher level of trust in Airbnb than large hotel chains. The sharing community has grown in part because consumers feel that the money they pay to these services is going to hard-working people just like them, their friends and neighbors, rather than to elite and wealthy executives.

How do you best and successfully engage activist shareholders, regulators, and the plethora of special interest groups in a way that does not cost your organization exorbitant amounts of your resources and when do you ignore them?

Consumers' opinions have merit and you must respond. In spring 2017, Alain Belemare, Bombardier's chief executive officer announced at a press release that he had asked the company's board of directors to defer 50 percent of their executive compensation until 2020. This announcement followed public protests outside of Bombardier offices and on social media. Bombardier's corporate headquarters are located in Montreal, Quebec, and the provincial government had provided $1 billion in taxpayers' money to assist Bombardier. The 2017 compensation for the chairman and five senior executives had been set at $32 million, an increase of $11 million from the prior year.

Activist Shareholders' Versions of the Truth

Shareholder activist and billionaire Carl Ichan has been active in business since the early 1980s. He started as a corporate raider, became involved in takeovers of pharmaceuticals in 2005 and proxy battles in 2010. His direct talk and free-wheeling actions appeal to a portion of North American audiences. His words particularly resonate with shareholders and consumers who remember the impacts of Enron and the global financial crisis as well as the excessive profit margins in pharmaceuticals. In 2013, US-based Pfizer was reported to have earned a profit margin of 42 percent, more than 20 percent higher than the average for the industry in an industry with margins that already well exceed most others, except for banks.

http://bbc.com/news/business-28212223

Ichan has little sympathy for CEOs, whom he believes are not taking the difficult actions they need to take or are somewhat absent on the job. He laments boards of directors not taking a tougher stance and holding CEOs accountable. His comments include describing organizations as "bloated with heavy bureaucracies and rampant waste... [and claims that he and others can] go into companies and knock off 30 percent of waste... [denigrates] fat CEO paycheques and bonuses... [boards of directors] give them all this money even when they are doing a terrible job." Ichan has a metaphor "that the guy that gets in and moves up the ladder… the guy you like… a buddy… he does not make waves… that is the guy that moves up the ladder in the corporate world and becomes CEO… too often boards do not hold management's feet to the fire."

As a board chair, here is what Randy Findlay does to proactively manage shareholders, "If you make a good case with your institutional shareholders, you have a chance. They will hear from the activists but you have to be there before. That's hard and there is a ton of back and forth." Tell them that "the chair is available, not forceful but we are here, we are open if you want to have a conversation." Open the door. A number of them have said "we want to talk to you." One group asked about strategy, "we want to know about the process, how involved you are and how you select your board members?" A really good question they asked was, "who is the most dominant board member?" My response was "On what subject? We have a vice chair of a national bank so if you want to talk about capital markets we are going to David. If you want to talk about compensation we have someone who has seen the most compensation and he chairs the committee. If you want to talk governance we have Leslie O'Donoghue. We don't have one dominant member."

The characteristics Ichan attributes to CEOs and boards are found in organizations of all sizes and in every industry. In addition, within Fortune 1000 companies, the characteristics of entitlement, resistance to change, and a lack of diversity can be deeply entrenched in middle management as well. In large organizations, CEOs are often unaware of the degree to which middle management are invested in the status quo and resisting changes that put their perceived security, compensation, or influence at risk.

You can see the difference between CEOs, executives, emerging leaders and new leaders in an organization. You can see the ones that are continuously seeking to improve versus those saying

"OK I arrived, this was my destination. Now here I am." "I'm good enough." Well you are not, because tomorrow is going to be different than yesterday and you are going to be left behind.

—Luc Desjardins

Sharon Ludlow describes the journey to engaging all stakeholders in more diverse thinking.

We used the expression "thinking globally" rather than just diversity. And global was not defined by geography. Inclusion was promoted ahead of diversity. Part of the global thinking mantra was asking 'have you been inclusive enough to consider the input or the criticism of all of the stakeholders, whether they were internal or external in order to get to your end solution?' That's part of promoting inclusion over just diversity.

When people made recommendations, we would ask, 'Have you thought about all of the aspects of what it is we're about to do?' It was important to not simply use the word diversity because that often implies only gender, which was not at all what we were trying to achieve. 'Let's think globally,' meant that you've considered everything. You've considered all aspects. You've considered the internal impact to your part of the organization and the perspective of the whole organization. You've also considered the entire marketplace around you. Global thinking meant that you have considered all angles, so sort of a multi-dimensional lens on your initiative.

—Sharon Ludlow

Fortunately these problems are less common in small- to mid-sized organizations and you have the flexibility to operate without a traditional hierarchy of layers and silos. Suzanne West has created an organization structure that enables the flow of information, mitigates risk, and builds leaders on a daily basis. In addition, her structure and way of leading is creating an organic talent management and succession process for Imaginea Energy.

I have a very unique organizational model, basically we don't have any hierarchy. It's self-managing, self-character, self-mastery based. We teach everybody to be a leader. That's the good part of it, rather than having one of you as designated leader. We teach everybody to be a leader and then they step up when they need to be a leader within their area of expertise, within their strengths or as a public leader. [In this environment] you need to know when to follow because that is the right thing to do at the top.

—Suzanne West

Luc Desjardins puts himself in the mind of an activist and approaches running his business as if he was the activist. He shared his perspective on how he would or has handled conversations with activists and his board.

Before I go back to work [after a holiday] I ask myself "What would you see if you were just coming in? What did not go well for me and us this year and how will I do things better? What is it that we are missing and what should we do about that?" I start from scratch every year. As an activist, you are transparent. You look closely at the company and look to improve it. If you don't look at it like that, you don't see what you could be doing. We are willing to be the best operator in costs compared to others in our industry. I am developing marketing and sales differentiation. I am investing in technology. I am investing in talent.

[I would ask the board and any activist] "So what am I missing? Maybe something. You want to come here and make more profit, how will you do that?"

The activist is going to come in and milk it. I don't want to do that. The activist can make more money for the company next year. I want to make more money three and five years from now. If we have a disconnect and the activist can convince the board and everybody else that we should strive for [big results over] the next twelve months with this activist, then come on in then. That's what should happen. I will go run another company that fits my culture, values and how I think it will be run.

I am not very afraid of activists. When I encounter a CEO who's afraid of activists, that worries me.

—Luc Desjardins

Exercise #5—Taking the activist view from within

Score each question below: 1=Rarely; 3=Sometimes; 5=Often

How often do you directly receive suggestions or innovative ideas from employees who do not report directly to you?	
How often do your direct reports present ideas that they have heard from staff? This can include new approaches to existing processes, new products, improvements to services, or improved use of technology?	
How often do you speak one-on-one or with small groups of employees to gather their feedback?	
How frequently do you inject new talent from the outside, particularly in management roles and with experience from another industry?	
How often do you introduce new technology, not large-scale programs but collaboration tools such as Google, Skype, or zoom and communication tools internally and externally including video, Twitter, or other appropriate social media?	
Do you conduct an employee engagement survey and even more importantly, do you implement changes based on employee feedback and govern these changes to ensure that they are sustained?	
Do you conduct 360 degree surveys for management staff at least every two years?	

Score each question below: 1=Not at all; 3=Somewhat; 5=Very much

Is your compensation clearly grounded in pay for performance? Rather than—pay for tenure, for prior experience, for actions completed during the year, for the fact that it was "a very busy year."	
Is any incentive compensation, that is, bonus, calculated to include at least 25% of the bonus attributable to company results?	

Do you and your team leverage external expertise and implement what you learn from—speakers, facilitators, new business books, or articles?	
Do you evaluate your employees for capability and potential and identify your future managers and specialists?	
If yes to the above question, do you utilize formal development plans for all employees including marginal and well-placed employees?	

Evaluation

60 perfect score: You are in the top 5 percent of companies. Keep up the great work and never rest on your laurels. Keep asking yourself, your employees, and your customers "what can we be doing better? What should we stop doing?"

48 to 60: You are in the top 10 percent of companies. This score indicates that you are fostering ideas and innovation, engaging and developing your people, and demonstrating solid leadership performance. Pick one item that you scored a 1 or 3 and develop one plan of action to commence within one week.

30 to 47: You are sitting squarely with many of your competitors. You can benefit greatly from making some changes. Pick two items on which you scored 1 or 3. Engage your management team. Commit to implementing these two items within 30 days. Communicate this commitment to your employees to hold yourself accountable. Ask yourself—do you have the right management team in place?

12 to 29: You have a large opportunity to improve your profit margins. You are missing out on opportunities to strengthen your brand, increase your ROI, reduce costs, and engage your employees and likely your customers. You need to take action immediately and will benefit from external expertise.

In the words of Carl Ichan: "The CEO is getting a huge bonus and didn't do anything and the earnings are bad... why aren't we making this guy accountable?" https://video.search.yahoo.com/search/video?-fr=spigot-chr-gcmac&p=carl+ichan+youtube#id=3&vid=8e8d7279f-8c4263961563520675b130f&action=clicka_t

Hold yourself and your management team accountable. Your employees and customers are counting on you.

It is worth noting that while Carl has uncovered waste and arrogance in many situations and has increased value for the shareholders, it is not always the case that a targeted company has been poorly managed. In the case of Talisman Energy, as Carl entered into deeper conversations with then CEO Hal Kvisle, he discovered that sometimes it is not quite as simple to resolve as he first believed, nor is the board and executive operating as poorly as he may have postulated.

Responding to Say on Pay

Your company may or may not be large enough to warrant requesting a say on pay from your shareholders. Even if you are not of the size and scale to participate, it is beneficial to understand the trends and the implications for all CEOs.

The Hay Group, now part of Korn Ferry, regularly provides market information on this topic. Boards are paying greater attention to CEO compensation with the advent of shareholder votes on CEO pay. A high percentage approval in one year does not guarantee a high approval rating in subsequent years. Most Fortune 500 companies have been receiving approval but there are some notable exceptions; shareholders are paying attention. Oracle received only 46 percent approval in 2014. In 2012, Citigroup did not have shareholder support and Abercrombie and Fitch lost its vote for consecutive years until they made changes to their compensation practices.

This trend has resulted in more organizations increasing the proportion of compensation related to performance. Based on a Hay survey, performance-based share awards is the largest piece of long-term incentives; use of stock options and restricted shares is declining.

http://fortune.com/2015/07/08/say-on-pay-ceos/

What does this mean for you? If your shareholder proxy includes say on pay, then you are already well aware and may have seen changes within your firm. If you are a smaller organization or privately held, there are lessons here for you as well. Employees are shareholders, perhaps not of your company but at others. Increased transparency to executive compensation has heightened expectations of consumers and employees. 360 degree leaders are comfortable with transparency. They are ethical and open to being challenged and held to account. Take a look at your behavior as a leader. Do you and your management team have perks that are not shared by employees? That is common, but do not develop an entitlement view on this; you may be challenged. Is your compensation and that of all management tied in part to the performance of the company? Is there a direct alignment to performance for management and all employees? If not, determine how you will put that in place in the next 12 months. It is the only sustainable choice in running a highly successful company.

This chapter must end on a positive note. One of the reasons for this book was to highlight the values driven, honorable CEOs and senior executives who operate across North America—particularly at a time when news (real or fake), activism, and social media often predominantly feature and sometimes inspire mistrust, misjudgment, and greed.

> There are heroes out there. I see them all the time. Seeing heroes or villains depends on where you turn your eyes to, what you're watching. If you watch the news, sure there's bad guys. But look around you; there are heroes all round. In regard to trust of our larger institutions, I'd change the question. Are those organizations more untrustworthy than they were 10-20 years ago or is it just the fact that we have social media or alternative news sites that give different perspectives? I don't think government or big businesses are less trustworthy than 10, 20, 50, or 100 years ago. If you are a student of history you see much was just hidden at the time; now there is greater transparency and generally it's a good thing. Yes, it can be misused but overall it's forced organizations to be more accountable.
>
> —Cal Yonker

CHAPTER 7

The Self-Aware CEO

Failure helps you learn very quickly. It is part of the necessary ingredient for growing quickly and transforming. Failure has got a bad rap and we avoid it like the plague; that means we avoid being spectacular as well.

—Suzanne West

I turned things down because it was a trade-off that I couldn't reconcile in the moment. The trade-off was too great in the moment. I couldn't figure out a way to do what I knew was important personally to what was important professionally. And the personal whip won every time. So I am very proud of the fact that if I didn't think I could figure out how to make it work, I did choose the personal and I took the risk that my career would not go anywhere. And ironically, it actually in many ways gave me more credibility. It strengthened what people thought of me because I was willing to make choices. And it actually increased their respect for me. So what I thought was going to be dead ends turned out to be Supreme Court stepping-stones.

—Gianna Manes

Don't Waste Your Life in the Waiting Room

An estimated 70 percent of people have said that they postpone living their most preferred life until their parents have passed. With average life expectancies of 80+ years in North America, some adults are sacrificing decades of potential greater vitality, enjoyment, and fulfillment. In other cases, people supplant their interests or goals in response to pressure from spouses or even grown children. The following are a few examples.

Janet Francis* was a successful senior executive who was highly regarded for her contributions in retail banking and as a director for several not-for-profit agencies. In business, she consistently delivered strong financial performance and held a reputation as a highly collaborative and inspiring leader. She was married with a daughter in secondary school when she told me that she "hated" the house they have lived in for nine years. Her husband was somewhat indifferent to where they lived, so she acquiesced and stayed living in a house that she said made her miserable while living there.

*name changed

Tyler Rankin*, CEO of a large telecom company, had an entrepreneurial streak and was quite intrigued by the idea of joining a startup. He had the business savvy and technical aptitude to pursue several opportunities. His father had worked for a blue chip company for 37 years and had challenged Tyler by saying, "these days, there are very few CEOs who can last in their job more than four years." At 57 years of age, Tyler wanted to prove to his father that he was one of the exceptions and so deferred the entrepreneurial opportunities that were presented to him; waiting until the day he felt he could follow his own path.

*name changed

Sometimes we remain in the waiting room for financial reasons—we stay where we are to ride out an economic downturn, to secure long-term incentive compensation, to pay for children's private school, to save for college tuition or because we think we feel a responsibility to our family to ensure continuity of current compensation. That may be the appropriate decision for a period of time, but I recommend no longer than three to five years. No financial situation or market condition is permanent. If you are not fully engaged in your role, have lost your enthusiasm, or know you really want to strive for something new, do not overthink it and do not wait. Risk taking is a hallmark of 360 degree CEOs. When passion wanes, performance stalls and the decision may be made for you.

One of the best pieces of feedback I ever received from an external coach was this, "Lorraine, when you get bored, it is not a good thing." Cal Yonker cited this as well.

"I find my passion wanes when times are good. I have a great team that I work with. When it's good and they are executing, their need for me is less. I find myself bored and less passionate. Reflecting on that question, that was a surprising revelation that I found."

Multitudes of executives successfully make career changes with few negative results.

If finances are an important consideration, undertake careful planning including a structured financial plan; it may be much more advantageous than you think. It is worth noting here that for 360 degree CEOs, money is not one of the primary or even secondary motivators. Money may have been more important earlier in their careers, to enable a desired lifestyle or as a metric of career performance. And they expect to be appropriately and equitably compensated. For these leaders, financial gain takes a back seat to creating and sustaining a corporate culture that is fulfilling and rewarding for many people. These leaders are motivated by: intellectual stimulation and challenges, delivering top line results, solving complex problems, having the freedom to lead a company in alignment with their values, and to grow an enterprise, organically or through acquisition. If you are in your current position primarily for the compensation, you are not yet a 360 degree executive. Make the changes required to your financial situation so that you can free yourself to achieve your full potential.

Sabbaticals and Personal Pursuits

Sometimes it takes only a small nudge and other times a more dramatic change to pursue a fresh path. While traveling in Cambodia and Vietnam, I met a 66-year-old woman from the United Kingdom. She had been working as a teacher when her husband passed away at age 60. During their life together, they restricted their travel to the continent, as he considered travel broader afield to be too adventurous. She opted for immediate retirement and in six years, had circumnavigated the globe twice and spent much of each year exploring and traveling. She determined that life could be much shorter than expected and she was going to make the most of it. Making many new friends across the globe has inspired her.

While exploring the Galapagos Islands, we met a terrific American family, a Florida couple with 13- and 9-year-old children. The husband had sold his business after several years of 70-hour workweeks. They wanted to re-establish their family relationships and expand their knowledge of the world and other cultures before their son entered secondary school and before the husband returned to employment. They had traveled to India, to introduce the children to their father's heritage and to far-flung family. When we met them, they had just completed eight weeks exploring South America. They were returning to Florida for Christmas, following which they would head to Australia and New Zealand. It was apparent the father would fully embrace a return to business, as he was a passionate entrepreneur and highly creative. In the meantime, they were building indelible memories while reinforcing their closely held values with their children.

And Janet Francis, the successful executive who did not like her house? After 11 years in the house she did not like, she seized an opportunity for a complex job in another city. She and her husband are enjoying their new locale; their daughter is in university and Janet is thriving personally and professionally.

Demonstrating Fearlessness

Alan Weiss, head of Summit Consulting Group, embodies someone who many years ago took charge of his life and limited spending time in what I call the "waiting room." Alan's father lived well into his 90s, by which time his son had seized life in what he considers a fearless manner.

> My family was poor, poor to the point that my parents argued about how to pay the rent each month and the rent was $40... sometimes it was a matter of borrowing from a friend or a family member... pretty awful. I decided I never wanted to be in that position. When I regarded other people as less educated or less intelligent, I didn't give their opinions equal weight with my own. If they felt I shouldn't do something, who cares?

He cites the following benefits of charting his own path with his long-time spouse Maria:

> We got married and moved into a very expensive high rise [in NY city] that we could not really afford... but we did what we needed to and we made it work [in spite of] others saying that we never should have done it, but we developed this great circle of friends who were in the arts in NY, all by the age of 22.... It was wonderful because we did what we thought we could do and we did not listen to anyone else.

It may be an old adage but it remains true that we learn the most when addressing difficult situations.

> In terms of my overall development, it was the recessions that hit, the major changes in tech that caused problems within the company and being able to lead, manage and navigate throughout those time periods and coming out stronger and seeing competitors fall by the wayside [that was the most rewarding]. The proudest periods were when I look back over the past 20 years to what would be considered the low points by most standards and being able to come through those in stronger positions.
>
> —Cal Yonker

Building a life of our creation takes a certain amount of self-confidence and a willingness to take risk, particularly the willingness to risk not always having the approval of our parents, siblings or close friends. It is important both early on, for example, in our 20s, and throughout our lives to recognize that a 360 degree life is achieved through personal growth and change. If we are not awake and regularly checking in with ourselves and those we are closest to, we may be conducting an autopilot life.

"Am I still pursuing the life I want?" (as opposed to a life that has worked up until now but may not be what your heart desires or your aspirations require).

If the answer is yes, challenge yourself.

Is this evidenced through the choices you are making—on a daily basis? This includes the activities you are spending your time on, the friends you associate with and your leisure pursuits.

What about the major choices such as career options available to you and the location where you live?

Status quo may feel easier, but it can limit your achievements and your personal satisfaction over time. Alan and I spoke about those who demonstrate an attribute of fearlessness.

> They are not silly; they do not gamble; they are not foolhardy [the difference is] they do not fear public opinion, they are willing to lose, to fail and to have a setback and that willingness to not succeed all the time emboldens as they do not take it as a strike to their ego when things do not work out as they hoped.

Knocking Down the Walls that Limit Your Opportunities

I thoroughly believe that for most of us, it will not be the actions we took that cause regret but rather the choices we did not make, the options we did not pursue, and the roads that beckoned but we did not travel.

Can you feel a burr under your saddle? When you are quiet, is there a voice or an idea that beckons? What do you feel when you consider or explore that feeling? Exhilaration and excitement? Or anxiety and trepidation?

Sitting in the fictitious waiting room can be quite insidious. You may not want to make big changes, but there may be small, niggling compromises you are making.

Exercise #6—If I followed a dream....
If you knew you could not fail, if you had a signed guarantee, what is one interest or idea you would pursue?

- Invest your time or money in a startup?
- Take an extended holiday with your family?

- Start a business or relocate to a different part of the country?
- Try your hand at learning a musical instrument?
- Try surfing or paddle boarding, skiing, or return to soccer or basketball by joining a community team?
- Volunteer for a cause?
- Book a week's holiday in Paris?

It need not be a life-changing endeavor. It need not be high risk or adventurous. Taking action is the key to shifting you mentally and physically from a place of waiting, of comfort, of ease—to a fuller and richer life. In my experience, once people take that first step, barricades fall to the ground, and when I speak to them a few years later they can often pinpoint that first decision or action that led them to greater fulfillment.

The most common shackles are fear and responses from others that we are uncomfortable with. The fears include fear of not being successful, or ironically, of being successful and, as a result, how one's life will change. Most of us are so habituated to resist change that we shy away from even positive change. Another common hindrance is the fear of other people's reactions—friends and family challenging us to ask why we are pursuing something different, why we are not content with the way things are, or suggesting that we will not be able to achieve the weight loss, secure the new job, enjoy living in the different city, working in a different industry, and so on. When influential people in our lives speak the words that echo our own insecurities, these doubts grow in size.

Susan Hill was an intelligent, ambitious executive at a pharmaceutical firm. She had a reputation as an insightful, compassionate leader and someone with enormous capacity to oversee many initiatives at one time. When we worked together, she was contemplating pursuing an executive MBA. As with most situations, she had undertaken her due diligence in selecting the best school and program for her requirements, had discussed it at length with her husband, and had the support of her leader and the board. At a company social event, she spoke with the husband of one of her executive team members. When they discussed her educational plans, he challenged her by saying, "I would love to pursue my MBA, but I just could not desert my children for 2 years." This struck a chord with her and ignited one of her worries, that the demands of her work and her ongoing pursuit of bigger jobs with more responsibility would be detrimental to her children. When we discussed this, her anxiety lessened when she agreed that his comments were most likely arising from his own decision to not pursue his education and that with her entrenched value and focus on family, her children would continue to thrive.

How Do You Quiet the Naysayers to Pursue a Life?

1. Know yourself.

   The CEOs and others that I highlight in this book all have a high degree of self-awareness. They have meaningful levels of self-confidence; this is required to lead others through challenging business cycles. They also listen carefully to feedback and incorporate what they hear to continually improve.

   > We conduct 360 degree surveys and actually I do one every year for myself. I send it to 30 to 40 of the management team. I start again as if from the beginning. When you do it on an annual basis, as a CEO, you're willing to learn through 360-degree evaluation. You're willing to look in the mirror and continue to learn about yourself, versus hiding from what the feedback might be. They [are free to] say what they want. I send a copy to the board. In our corporate survey we score 9.5 on transparency and communication. I never expected it to be that high.
   >
   > —Luc Desjardins

2. Get to know yourself better.
   - Utilize a structured 360 degree survey.
     - Many organizations utilize these. If yours does not, consider utilizing a proprietary survey to gather feedback.

When I engage with clients I utilize a set of structured questions and interviews. This is sometimes conducted in addition to or in lieu of online surveys.

o Important: Don't conduct a survey or gather and provide feedback without engaging a third party to facilitate an objective, external, and professional debrief of your results.

A large Fortune 500 company invested millions of dollars in annual surveys over a decade. Executives and managers received their results in an online report. They were encouraged to "review and share these results with your leader." There was no formal mechanism to track how frequently this happened or what percentage of participants reviewed their results with their leaders. There was no governance process to see how often development plans were created in response to the information contained in the survey feedback.

Contrast this with another Fortune 500 company who also invests millions of dollars in formalized 360 degree surveys. In this second case, the company utilizes external advisors to debrief individual results with each executive and manager. These advisors discuss potential blind spots, discuss how to leverage strengths and prepare executives for discussions with their manager, and prepare the CEO of this multibillion dollar company for a discussion with his executive leadership team and potentially with his board. They also track preparation of development plans for all management and review development against objectives for all high-potential employees. (For more on how best in class companies create a culture of accountability and develop their best performers, see my book *Feet to the Fire: How to Exemplify and Create the Accountability that Creates Great Companies*, Business Expert Press 2016).

In the second case, the company receives compounding ROI on their investment. In the first case, the results vary. When executives take the lead and ask their direct reports to review and discuss the survey results, there is some benefit. For those executives who also create a development plan aligned to the survey results, there is a greater benefit and ROI. However, it is not what it could be.

- Ask others for feedback—colleagues, direct reports, industry peers, others you know through volunteering, and so on.
  - Ask them specifically what they think you are particularly good at and what are 1 to 2 things you can improve upon in your interactions with others, or as demonstrated in your decisions, when managing a crisis, and so on.
- Listen carefully to the feedback from any naysayers.
  - Assess whether it contains any value or nuggets of wisdom. If yes, extract the value and make a change. If there is no discernable value, let it go and move on. If it bubbles up again and you find yourself thinking about it, unless you have received similar feedback from someone else, remind yourself that you have moved on and refuse to dwell on it or pursue that line of thinking.
  - I have sometimes observed talented people distracted more by the one person who is resistant to their leadership and/or has provided negative feedback than by their quieter supporters. If you find yourself reacting in this way, reach out to your supporters—the people who consistently believe in you.

Remind yourself that you can always settle for less, you can always change course, and you can always change your mind. So why not pursue what is possible?

What is one action you can take to release whatever shackles may be holding you back?

Exercise #7—Freeing yourself to move forward

- Get a fresh notebook or pad of paper. Write down situations in which you took a risk or made a choice that may have differed from prevailing wisdom or the expected path. Recognize your success. Recognize what you learned through that process. Realize that failures were not fatal and may have led to new growth.

- Write a list of all the things you are afraid of. Look at them in the cold light of day. You will discover that many of them can be overcome with planning. Other fears are outside of your control. Let them go.
- Complete a financial plan. Get your finances in line so that overspending or a burden of debt will no longer hold you back.
- Engage your spouse, partner, or a friend in your plan.
- Engage a financial planner or an external coach to assist if appropriate.

When the wind in one's sails is generated from authenticity, confidence, health, and vulnerability, you better navigate storms and attain speed in calm waters.

Your Legacy Started Years Ago

"Keep your eyes on the prize" is a common refrain (derived from a folk song during the US Civil Rights Movement 1950s). While organizations need an inspiring vision and overarching purpose, don't lose sight of the legacy you have already formulated by virtue of your choices and decisions to date. Furthermore, "where do you see yourself in five years?" is an outdated and potentially limiting question. Are you proud of what you have achieved to date? If not, start to make changes now. If you have rather narrowly defined your career epitaph, tear it up. Think instead of what is possible. "My father says, 'Mayo haven't you done enough?' You start thinking about it, you think, 'Gosh I thought I was just getting started. I went through all that training and those experiences and hard knocks to prepare...' As I think back about the last 30 years of my career the best ten are ahead."

I think the biggest surprise in a career is the career... As I think back to high school and university, I just thought, "you get out of university, you get a job, you work your entire life and you hope you make enough to pay your bills." Now I realize, we [most of us] could never have anticipated not only what we would be doing today, but the effects of what we are doing and the people that we affect and the circumstances by which we have come to be in the places we're in. I just look back and think, "this would have been completely unpredictable…" go back 30 years and tell me that you would have known that you would be doing what you're doing today and be where you're at.

—Mayo Schmidt

Rose Laboucan was chief at Driftpile First Nation for a dozen years. The first time she was nominated, her husband, also a band chief, encouraged her to run in the election out of respect for those who had nominated her. Rose led her band for over a decade, creating a sustainable legacy. A woman band chief was unusual in 2004 and remains so today. All of the council members who reported to her were men. When faced with leadership challenges, she always did so with the long view to what she wanted to accomplish as a leader and for her people.

In her early days as chief, she considered pursuing a manufacturing facility for their area. With her trademark transparency, she admitted that it was not initially viable as the facility would not be able to recruit and retain enough reputable employees. Drug and alcohol abuse was an issue. Consistent with highly successful leaders, Rose did not let the existing situation discourage or impede her from creating a different future. By 2016 she spoke with pride of the Rhodes scholar in their band and the reduction in drug and alcohol abuse.

Rose's tenacity in creating her legacy is laudable. For several years, not weeks or months, but years, she modeled the leadership behaviors that she wanted from her council members, believing that eventually she would create a positive change. She was always on time for meetings and thoroughly and completely prepared for all discussion or debate. She was well-educated, candid, respectful, and demonstrated integrity in every conversation and interaction. Over time, her consistency created the positive change she was seeking. One of the council members said to his peers, "if Rose is always on time and fully prepared for the meetings, we can be too."

As chief, like most senior leaders, Rose spent considerable time away from family. She was absent from home about 70 percent of the time while her husband took care of the children and home. Of course she missed the time with family, but knew that she needed to be physically present at meetings and events to best serve her constituents and to achieve her legacy. She recognized and seized the unique opportunity afforded by her position to change perceptions, to alter dialogue with government and business, and to define a new future for her band and other bands across the country. When meeting Prince Charles, she advised him, when he returned home, to deliver a message to his mother, Queen Elizabeth—"we have unfinished business." He agreed to share her comments with her majesty. In 2012, when addressing the panel present at the Enbridge pipeline hearings, she told them, "I want to be honest with you. I do not trust the panel. Two of you are from Calgary. One of you is from Ontario," referencing and acknowledging the biases the panel members would have. Rose Laboucan's legacy is one of honesty, integrity, leadership, and tenacity.

Legacies are not always shimmering visions of beauty in the far off future. Many legacies are formed through the way we conduct ourselves and are built one decision and action at a time. Paul Kelly, CEO of First Calgary, describes a "near death experience" of his credit union in 2008 and his actions at the time to address the crisis—a situation of which few people have or had any knowledge.

At the height of the financial crisis, markets were frozen and capital unavailable. Even large, well-established entities such as IBM could not raise overnight capital. Business was halted. At First Calgary, they had lost money for a couple of months and the situation was very tense. If the public became aware of any financial institution struggling financially, panic would ensue and could result in a rush of withdrawals. Paul made a calculated decision to take a financial position predicated on interest rates falling. He received approval for his recommendation, even though few understood the complexities of hedging and other underlying principles.

His forecast was accurate; rates plummeted within a month of his action and rather than the bank losing money or even breaking even, they made sufficient profits to sustain the organization through the global downturn. His actions averted a severe outcome. In his words, he "did the right thing, managed the crisis and yet did so without causing what could have been a huge disruption in the organization." No one knew of this other than his controller at the time. He calculated the benefits and risk of involving others in his decision and demonstrated leadership courage by taking what he believed was the best decision for the company. He shouldered the responsibility.

Another highlight for Paul was the first time First Calgary was recognized as one of Canada's Best Managed Companies by Deloitte (they are now platinum winners, having been awarded over eight years consecutively). The entire management team traveled to the award ceremony. Here is the key to creating a legacy—as Paul said to me, "it wasn't as much what we did that year or the year before," it was the consistent decisions and actions to build a strong team and a strong company that led to the external recognition and validation of their success.

If you think you may want to sell your company in five years, start to increase the value today. If you hope for a promotion and/or to be CEO in 10 years, demonstrate the behaviors of a 360 degree CEO right now.

Your legacy is created and substantiated now and 10 minutes from now and tomorrow when you interact with your family, your employees, and your colleagues. You create a legacy every day through how you speak with people, how you behave in a crisis, and how you respond when someone makes a mistake.

CHAPTER 8

Disarming Fear

A formidable impediment to achieving your best as a CEO or leader can be fear. A lack of confidence in one's own abilities can cause leaders to play small. The limiting belief that one does not have the resources to handle a crisis or unanticipated results of one's choices leaves leaders standing at the back of the stage rather than stepping into the limelight. Learn how recognized leaders Giuliani and Merkel elevated their credibility when responding to crises.

Unlocking the Door to the Prisons in Your Mind

Fears fall into a variety of categories: limiting beliefs, rational/logical fears, and irrational fears that often include phobias.

Limiting Beliefs

You may believe that you are not an articulate communicator and, therefore, will not be able to influence the Board to make a strategic acquisition or that the CFO's performance issues are as a result of you expecting too much of him.

I have worked with many leaders who have doubted themselves and their capabilities—in spite of considerable evidence pointing to the contrary. When I tell CEOs this, they are often surprised. I recall a conversation with a brilliant and talented president of a mid-sized company. After several quarters of rapid growth, economic pressures and personnel issues altered the successful trajectory. The president had to make a number of difficult financial and people decisions. He was critically questioning his abilities, asking what he could have done to prevent the situation, worried that his clients were losing faith in his firm, and so on. When I asked him if he had heard of the imposter syndrome (coined by psychologists in the 1970s), he said he had not. He then asked if it was anything like his secret fear, "the Board Chair and one of the board members is going to enter my office and advise that they made a mistake when they hired me and have identified my successor?" Of course that is an example of imposter syndrome. He was not unique in harboring that fear.

When you attribute your successes—including your ease when interacting with others, your keen financial acumen, your unerring ability to stay ahead of the competition—to external factors unrelated to your decisions, actions, and capabilities, you are holding limiting beliefs. These may have been formulated in messages you heard as a child or hear now from colleagues or a spouse. Whatever the source, you will benefit from recognizing and beating down these messages, replacing them with more positive and compassionate messages in your head.

A Few Words on Guilt

Someone once said, "lift the cover on any working mother and you will find guilt." In my conversations with executives, I consistently encounter guilt more frequently with successful women than I do with successful men. I abhor contributing to gender or ethnic stereotypes but this is so prevalent, I feel it is important to acknowledge. It may be that women experience more guilt or it may be that they have become more adept at identifying it and developing successful strategies to overcome it.

Consistent with the characteristics of the best leaders, Gianna Manes and Colleen Abdoulah demonstrated vulnerability in providing articulate and well-thought-out perspectives on guilt.

> This is a raw subject. There's always that tinge of "was it the right thing to do?" I always wonder about the time with my family. I'm probably facing that now as my kids are [at an age

where they are] wanting me around less and less. Everyone says, "where did that time go?" A lot of that time went to me working and my dedication to my company. I often hear women say that they were better mothers because they were fulfilled by a career. I am not one of those people.

I can say I became a better leader. I gained an appreciation for others to be successful. It was less about me and it was about the success of my kids and I translated that to the success of my teams. And I really realized that I love that. I am motivated by the success of others. It became less about me and I became a much more effective leader. So I can say without doubt, being a mother or a parent has made me a better leader.

I know that my family has gained experiences and has opportunities and we've done things that without my career we would have never been able to do. I also know there's both sides to this trade-off. I try to make it up when I can.

As an experiment, I decided to give up guilt for Lent. As a joke I said "I should give up guilt because I've been apologizing to everybody" when it was particularly harried and busy. I put some parameters around it. I said "I'm going to say OK I felt guilty but I acted differently so I'm good, either because I had no choice or I want to do this other thing too. I'm going to lose the guilt. I'm going to stop sharing it around and adding it to the baggage of guilt. Then I was going to let it go." And it's probably the best time I ever had; it was free.

Now I try to say will I try to think ahead a little bit more and say "am I not going to look back and regret that I wasn't there or make that phone call." I'm not always successful on any given day, but it actually has helped a lot. It helps to put it in that perspective, that's helped a lot. I just want my kids to be good, happy and productive adults. Now that they know if I am OK with it they are like OK. In fact they're often more OK with it than I am.

—Gianna Manes

If you can live in a place of humility, you don't feel so guilty. You realize you're only responsible for you; you're not responsible for how everybody else is taking care of themselves or being responsible for themselves… I spent 30 years of my life believing "if I did this, then this would happen. And if I did that, this outcome would happen." Then I received some really strong spiritual messages that said "not your role; not your job. That's your ego." Staying in a place of humility has helped me manage guilt.

—Colleen Abdoulah

In every conversation with highly successful CEOs, they willingly shared their regrets, their experiences with guilt, and their mistakes. Many of them shared the past fears that they have overcome. There is a correlation between these qualities of vulnerability and their ability to lead large organizations and people to achieve outstanding results.

Fear comes, I believe, from not being humble enough to really be authentically who you are. When I was based in my insecurities and trying to act like I knew things I didn't know or be a certain way, I was fearful a lot. "What if I was found out? What if they knew I wasn't really good at that or I didn't really know that?" I acted like I did; that caused fear.

When I negotiated for the job (at WOW), I had to meet a second private equity group and pass their inspection before the final offer. I flew to Boston and was feeling my insecurities. We started the interview, they're asking me what my plans are, how I will turn [the company] around. And I said, "I need to tell you guys right up front. There are two places I'm not really great. Here's what I'm really good at. I'm really good at leadership. I'm really good at people management and development. I'm really good at operations. I'm good at marketing, and I'm good at understanding the customer. What I'm not really great at is mergers and acquisitions or high finance. I can run a P&L and I can manage a business. Bank restructuring and all that stuff is not my thing. And two, I know enough to know if my chief technical officer is bullshitting me but I'm not technical."

As I said that my heart was pounding. The first guy said, "No big deal. We're the finance guys. If we ever look at mergers, we're there to do the due diligence. We're there to help you, you run the operations, you tell us what, if it's a good investment or not but we'll do the numbers. So no big deal there, we'll get you a really good CFO." And the other guy said, "Technically, you don't need to know all that stuff; we don't know all that stuff. We'll just get a good Chief Technical Officer and we'll be great." And then the interview went on and I did it with such confidence even though my fear was just there. Why? Because I put that boogieman right out there. I put out what I was fearful about, and it was gone.

So that's now how I have lived my life. Whatever I'm scared about I'm just going to name it. It's being authentic about your fears, being vulnerable. Because what I really found at WOW is that when I stood in front of employees and said, "Here's what you've got in me and here's what you don't have and here's what I need from you," they trusted me. And it not only garnered trust, it helped them be authentic, it helped them say, "I'm scared" or "I don't know" or "I need help" because they saw me modeling that.

—Colleen Abdoulah

Humility is an honorable characteristic, but not if it is holding your organization back from prudent risks or innovation. I have often advised leaders, "When you doubt yourself, it generates lesser outcomes." Identify realistic gaps in your capability, experience, or performance. Heed feedback from your direct reports, clients, or board members. Then establish one to two actions you can take to close the gaps and improve your performance. This can include recruiting people with complementary skills, attending executive development programs at an accredited university, or retaining an executive coach. In some cases, your board chair can be an excellent mentor and guide.

"Imposters" on Your Team?

I have advised executives that, interestingly, some of their best performers are often some of their most insecure people—leaders who are consistently striving to prove their worth to themselves through high levels of performance. For many years, the ambitions of a now highly successful CEO of a multinational company were fueled by his father telling him he would never rise from his part-time job during university to the top job. He did just that through 25+ years of hard work and stellar performance. What star performers do you have on your team who will benefit from recognition of both their achievements and their capabilities?

Rational Fears

These fears are logical and may be founded in experience. For example, I have coached executives terminated from an organization when they demonstrated reluctance to accept a new challenging assignment and others who had opted to stay in a less than satisfying situation rather than risk making an industry change. These executives' choices, perhaps seemingly well thought-out, produced opportunity costs for the individuals and organizations. We will evaluate this more in the section ahead.

Irrational Fears

If you are afraid of contracting cancer and you have a related family history, your fear may be well placed. If you are afraid of drowning, live in the Midwest and avoid all seaside destinations, your fear is ill-placed. If you or a close friend or family member have ever suffered anxiety disorders, you know how debilitating fear can be, even when it is not well-founded.

Many have found the following exercise beneficial. First, set aside 20 minutes of uninterrupted time. Find a fresh note pad or notebook and a pen that you like to write with. Refrain from using technology. We are at our most creative when writing by hand rather than typing. You can use a whiteboard in your office if you have privacy.

Exercise #8—Facing your fear

1. Create a list

Brainstorm a list of fears that you have—all that you can think of. If the ideas stop flowing after three or four minutes, don't complete the exercise prematurely. Give yourself another minute or two. You may be surprised what you come up with. I have provided a sample list here from clients.

List of fears
- Life-threatening illness
- Identified as a fraud; being found out to not have the skills for the job
- Being terminated
- Marital or relationship breakdown
- Child in trouble with the law
- Financial hardship or bankruptcy
- Natural disaster, fire, flood, tornado, earthquake, and so on
- Not enough time with your children, spouse, other family members
- Not telling a parent or loved one how you feel about them until it is too late
- Staying in a job too long
- Negatively impacting employees' lives through employment changes
- Being influenced to make unethical decisions
- Your company will not be acquired for the value you are expecting
- Dishonest employees
- Safety incidents or fatalities on your watch
- Regulatory snafus
- Loss of public reputation

2. Take stock

For each item on your list, categorize it as a fear you can influence (I) or out of your control (O).

Fear	"Influence-able" (I) or beyond control (O)
Life-threatening illness	I
Identified as a fraud; being found out to not have the skills for the job	I
Being terminated	I
Marital or relationship breakdown	I
Child in trouble with the law	I
Financial hardship or bankruptcy	I
Safety incidents	I
Natural disaster, fire, flood	O

3. Score the risk

Some fears are more likely to occur than others. For example, as CEO, if you have a deteriorating relationship with your board chair, your fear of being terminated may be valid. If you live in the Midwest, the fear of earthquake is highly unlikely. Score each item as 1: unlikely, 2: medium risk, or 3: high risk. For high risk items—note why.

4. Take action

For every influence-able fear, identify at least one action you can take. This can include: scheduling a check-up with your physician; scheduling a regular date night with your spouse; or making an appointment with your financial planner to improve your financial health.

Fear	I/O rating	Score 1, 2, or 3	Why	Comment
Life-threatening illness	I	3	-Overweight -Smoking -High blood pressure	-Schedule check-up with physician. -Hire a personal trainer or a nutritionist. -Join a gym and commit to a workout schedule with a friend.

Identified as a fraud; being found out to not have the skills for the job	I	1		-Conduct feedback for you and your team. Model leadership behavior by creating a development plan to leverage your strengths and address gaps.
Being terminated	I	1		-Re-establish your network. -Ask yourself honestly if you are satisfied with your job. If not, what needs to change?
Marital or relationship breakdown	I	2		-Have a heart-to-heart with your partner. -Schedule regular date nights. -Book a trip away from day-to-day responsibil-ities.
Child in trouble with the law	I	1		-Speak honestly with your child and share your fears. -Ask friends and health care provider for referral to a counselor.
Financial hard-ship or bank-ruptcy	I	1		-Book an appointment with a financial planner. -Meet with your banker. -Consolidate debt.
Safety incidents	I	2		-Review results year to date (YTD) and trends year over year (YOY) and quarter over quarter. -If your fears are affirmed, hire expertise to conduct safety audits.
Natural disaster, fire, flood, tornado, earthquake	O and I	1		-You cannot control Mother Nature. You can establish or update your company's disaster recov-ery plan and business continuity actions. -Review your home and auto insurance and make adjustments if warranted.

Fear is instinctual and can serve as a lifesaving mechanism. We all carry some level of fear. When it is leveraged to guide risk analysis before making an important decision that may affect share price, customers, employees, or market share, it can be useful. When the fear erects a door that inhibits us from taking any action that may fail, it can be prohibitive. Once you have shone the light of day on your fears and generated a list of preventative actions, where appropriate, it frees you to move forward. It also opens you and your organization to new and unlimited possibilities.

Trials by Fire

In December 2001, *Time* magazine named Rudy Giuliani its Person of the Year. Interestingly, prior to 9/11, Giuliani's public image was that of a rigid, self righteous, and ambitious politician. Following 9/11, he was elevated to a leader who united citizens of a city, while facing their greatest ever crisis. When asked how he knew what to do and what to say during the horrifying hours and days, Giuliani said that he felt ill-equipped to respond. He reached for speeches and writings of Winston Churchill to learn what the British leader had done during WWII and the bombings of London. Churchill was a reticent speaker who suffered from depression and yet inspired hundreds of thousands and generated hope. We can see evidence of Churchill's influence in public statements made by Giuliani, "Tomorrow New York is going to be here… and we're going to rebuild, and we're going to be stronger than we were before… I want the people of New York to be an example to the rest of the country, and the rest of the world, that terrorism can't stop us."

On March 24, 2015, Germanwings flight 4U 9525 crashed in the French Alps. In response, German Chancellor Angela Merkel immediately turned her attention to the tragedy. At a press conference, Merkel called it "a shock that puts us in Germany and the French and Spanish in mourning." Her swift action was consistent with her approach in all difficult situations faced by Germany and on the continent. Merkel, Germany's first female Chancellor has often been described as the de facto leader of the European Union, in response to her forthright, courageous approach, and demonstrated confidence, even when she may be fearful inside.

You need not be in the top job to demonstrate leadership in challenging situations.

> I wasn't even the CEO but the head of a business unit… we were in tons of debt and we had been spun out from TransCanada and we knew it was a lousy deal and… that was really difficult and we had to lay off people and we had to cut back salaries. It was not happy, but we treated everybody very well, as best we could. We did all that and still now I have people come say, "even though you had to lay me off I still think you are the best boss I ever had because then I went on to do this and that." Someone once said "when you can walk down the street and you don't have to worry about walking to the other side because you don't know who you're going to meet, that's pretty rewarding in your career."
>
> —Randy Findlay

Anchors for the Storms

Now that you have cast daylight on the monsters in the closet, you will move ahead with a lighter burden. This will enable a heightened ability to achieve results consistent with your potential. Sometimes, we are presented with difficult situations that require us to draw on our own reserves—a life-threatening illness, a child in trouble with the law, or a family member or close friend with psychological issues or substance abuse. Or you may be faced with a difficult business challenge such as a hostile or unwelcome acquisition, a brand-damaging customer error, economic storms, and so on. In those situations, you will best weather the storms by securing yourself to the anchors in your life.

If you have little familiarity with sailing, you may be surprised to learn that sailors often disagree about the best anchor. Why? Because depending on the conditions of the water and the lake or sea bottom, the wrong anchor may not set or may secure but later drag, risking injury. Similarly, when facing threatening and difficult situations, leaders' preferences and requirements for the best support systems may vary considerably. When you identify and tie to the best anchors, you will better weather the storms. This is particularly important when you are leading others. As you are stronger and feeling more secure, you will lead from a position of strength and everyone will benefit.

Anchors can be people or actions that strengthen your resilience, increase your confidence and self-belief, and make you stronger.

Anchors

- Spouse, friend, colleague, board chair, or member of your management team who has your back, believes in you, listens without judgment.
- Exercise, sleep, meditation, prayer, sports, the beach, the mountains, music, art, culture, entertaining, and so on.

In business, you will be faced with imposed or self-initiated stressful situations.

Imposed and/or Potentially Threatening Situations

- Organizational missteps (oil spills; environmental damage; employee fatality; fraud; insider trading; or a sexual harassment charge). Consider VW's emissions debacle; fatalities attributed to GM's ignition failures; the BP oil spill; or Turing Pharmaceutical's 5,000 percent increase in drug price.
- Loss of customers, market share
- Financial losses
- New, capable, and large competitor(s)
- Fees or charges imposed for regulatory noncompliance
- Employee or contractor injury or fatality
- Fire or theft

Self-Initiated Changes

When you have initiated the change, it is often easier to accept and lead. You understand the rationale for the change, you are likely orchestrating the change, and you may be inspired and excited about the process and/ or the resulting benefits. As a result, the fear factor may be mitigated.

However, while this is the case, I often counsel leaders to trust their judgment and take action. Concern for others' reactions, while considerate, should not delay your plans.

Typical examples of self-initiated changes include:

- Potentially unpopular changes to your management team, for example, terminating a well-liked leader
- Making an acquisition
- Divesting part of the business
- Outsourcing part of the operations
- Stopping a product or service offering
- Relocating corporate or field offices

Whether imposed or self-initiated changes, the best anchors are others who will:

- Hold you accountable for taking action in a timely manner.
- Empathize with your concern for others' reactions and then move you forward.
- Play devil's advocate.
- View your actions through a different lens, for example, someone whose strengths are different from and complement your own.
- Remember the action-oriented anchors that are the best sources of your stress release—exercise, nutrition, sports, arts, entertainment, and so on. Now is the time to draw on these more than ever.

Life Issues

- Illnesses—spouse, children, or self
- Aging parents
- Substance abuse—family member or good friend
- Marital breakdown
- Your own emotional baggage
- Spouse with gambling or other addiction

When facing life issues, the ideal anchors are others who will:

- Listen and empathize
- Provide referrals and introductions to professionals with the specialized expertise you require
- Others who have successfully overcome similar challenges.

Stay away from martyrs or masochists who will relish in wallowing. Seek out those who believe in positive action and life affirming choices.

Whether you are responding to business challenges, creating a new world order for your firm or buffeted by life challenges, de-isolate yourself by connecting with your trusted advisors and appropriate professionals. Ideally you have at least a small composite of people you can draw on. Be open to seeking new sources of expertise depending on the situation.

Testing the Market

Remember when you were a child, huddled under the covers, wondering if there was something scary under your bed? Or entering your bathroom as a young adult, after watching a horror flick, and staring with unease at the closed shower curtain? When you mustered up the courage to peer under the bed, or whipped back the shower curtain to see the empty space, the fears evaporated. It is the same with facing the fears that may be holding us back from making career decisions.

Suzanne Franklin founded and ran a successful logistics company. Over several years, she encountered many ups and downs in her life and business. One of her children has Down syndrome; she, her mother and sister all faced cancer; she moved across the country; and she and her husband divorced. Her company grew rapidly and then had to scale back for a period of time, terminating some of their employees. She faced the troughs of struggling to make payroll and then the highs of selecting from a number of financial suitors such as Goldman Sachs offering multimillions of dollars. She recognized that her partners from company inception no longer had the skills to run the larger organization and long-time friendships dissolved.

She was highly effective at establishing and drawing on anchors. She hired someone to help her change her nutrition to best respond to colon cancer. She sought out the counsel of other CEOs who had obtained financing from the large firms before making her decision. She drew on my expertise to re-build the leadership team and to develop a new vision and strategy for the organization. Playing golf and the social interaction during the game picked her up after even the toughest days and weeks. Knowing this, whenever she could she joined the weekly Nine and Dine, even and particularly when she was tired and the work was piled high. She recognized that she was a better leader and a healthier person when she secured herself to the anchors in her life on a consistent and fit-for-purpose basis.

Joe Natale, former CEO of TELUS, forfeited the top job at the telecommunications firm after only four quarters. When he accepted the senior position he committed to moving from Toronto to Vancouver, Canada within three years. When he decided that his family would not be in a position to relocate for several years, the board accepted his resignation. During Mr. Natale's reign, TELUS experienced strong financial results with over $10 billion in annual revenues. The announcement surprised analysts and the market, as there had been no indicators of dissatisfaction from top executives or boards.

While only those closest to Mr. Natale know the process he undertook to arrive at his decision, we can presume that while quite possibly a difficult decision, once made and communicated, he was in a position to move forward. His choice was an uncommon one for a male executive in any country or industry and may have been rooted in his personal values.

Satisfaction Plateaus

It is not uncommon for executives to reach a satisfaction plateau in their careers. A founder and CEO may realize her long ago vision for her company. A hired gun CEO, having successfully elevated an organization from near financial ruin or reputational damage to a position of financial strength and a healthy goodwill on the balance sheet, may no longer experience the same rush of exhilaration when entering the office.

When I advise leaders in these situations, what surprises me is how little awareness the executives have of the multiple possibilities available to them. In some cases, they attribute the organization's success to external factors such as market conditions, weak competitors, or growing overseas demand. Or they recognize their contribution to the corporate results but minimize their ability to transfer the strategies and leadership behaviors to another industry or geography from public to private company.

High achievers and highly intelligent professionals find it challenging to independently identify the specific traits, behaviors, and to a lesser degree, actions and decisions, attributable to their success. The following exercise is effective at teasing out the underlying contributions.

Exercise #9—Uncovering the gems

Step 1

Identify three to five material corporate or divisional successes from the last three to five years, for example, increased profitability, reduced employee turnover, greater market share, improved EBITA.

Step 2

Consider—what actions did you take or decisions did you make that contributed to these results?

Step 3

Identify two to three professional achievements of the past 10 years, for example, completed executive MBA, undertook difficult and courageous decisions such as exiting a market or terminating a direct report, or a glowing performance review.

Step 4

Viewing these results objectively, as if achieved by someone else—a colleague, friend, or direct report, identify three to five strengths you would attribute to this individual. Do these apply to you? If so, make note of them. If not, what other strengths (drawn on experience and natural abilities) contributed to these achievements. Write them down.

Step 5

Share this exercise with a spouse, colleague, or direct report. Ask them to identify any achievements, talents, and capabilities you may have missed.

In the next section you will identify interests that will later be matched to skills.

Creating Your Interest Inventory

Complete the table below.

Area of interest	Personal interests	Why? What is the most captivating?	Identify commonalities
Books, movies, or TV shows that most interested you	• • •		
Most engaging hobbies or leisure activities	• • •		
Topics of interest in media, e.g., legal topics, agriculture, finance, economics, health	• • •		
Engaging volunteer activities and/ or causes, e.g., Humane Society, Habitat for Humanity, Room to Read	• • •		

As you review your answers, what commonalities can you identify? Make note of them in the third column.

Ron Harding was a well-respected senior executive of a large insurance company. When his firm was acquired by a large multinational, he opted for a severance package. After 26 years in the industry and having participated in several mergers, his curiosity had waned and he wanted to take the opportunity. While he enjoyed interacting with his industry peers and his breadth of responsibilities including the P&L

for North America, he recognized that his declining passion for the role was having a subtle but negative impact on his performance. Not yet 50 years old, Ron wanted to apply his intellect and energy to a challenging and rewarding role.

He was uncertain whether he would be accepted into a senior role in another industry. He considered starting a new company but felt he was best suited to a corporate role in an established firm. When completing assessments he identified the following themes: interest in science and innovation, regulatory expertise, a passion for holding P&L responsibility, and an interest and aptitude in government relations and stakeholder engagement. As he was still uncertain how these could fit together and for what industries they would apply, we developed a structured plan that included researching other industries and extensively networking.

Ron discovered that his capabilities were of interest to banks, technology firms, life sciences companies, and pharmaceuticals. He also discovered that his skills and interests were a great fit for the energy industry. He was appointed chief operating officer of a $3 billion company that provided storage and transportation services to the oil and gas industry. His regulatory and government-relations skills were of keen interest to the board and CEO. They were seeking a successor for the CEO within four years, allowing sufficient time for Ron to prepare. Ron was keen to learn and contribute to the innovative steps being undertaken to ensure environmental protection and health and safety.

Going to Market

Now It's Your Turn

Once you have completed the two exercises, what themes can you identify? Describe some ideal outcomes for yourself.

A banking executive responded, "I would most enjoy working in an industry that experiences volatility, has little regulatory oversight and is highly dependent on understanding customer preferences. In addition, I realize I am highly effective at generating profitable enterprises, even when margins are low." Retail could be a good fit in this scenario—and there are many options, such as luxury goods or consumer technology.

"For the past several years I have been CEO of a $20B asset management/property management company. I enjoy the commercial clients, the prestige and cachet of interacting with companies across the globe." For this individual, a role in the hospitality industry for an organization such as Taj Group of luxury hotels could be an interesting next opportunity.

Undertaking Your Due Diligence

Executive recruiters with global firms such as Korn Ferry, Boyden, and Egon Zehnder can be useful in providing market information, compensation, and industry updates. As an executive, you may have an established relationship with one of these firms if you have used their services. If not, it is worth an investment of your time to build relationships with two or three of the partners. Their reputation is dependent on maintaining confidentiality, which is of upmost importance to you as well. Recruiters are most applicable when you want to make a change within your industry. They are compensated to fill positions with the best-fit candidates as quickly as possible, so are not always the best sources when changing industries, and/or if you cannot clearly articulate your next best role.

Your greatest asset is your network. Trusted colleagues are an excellent source of information. As you consider whom you can confidently speak with, ask yourself the following:

- Who can I be assured will keep any discussion confidential?
- Who has experience in different industries, through their participation on boards or in executive positions?
- Who has successfully made a career change, for example, a geographical move, changed companies or industries?
- Who is well connected and always acts as a source of introductions to others?

Now you are ready to approach the market. Gather your information—your identified strengths and areas of interest, the industries you are interested in (and how you would make a meaningful contribution) and the list of people you will speak with. As an executive with a demanding job, it requires discipline to allocate time for this process. Split the tasks into manageable pieces and make time in your calendar. Complete at least one action every week.

A client had spent many successful years in professional services in Europe. By his mid-40s his interest was waning. He determined a fresh start with a new firm would provide the resurgence he was seeking. Moving firms when you are a partner is not insignificant. He successfully transitioned to another global firm, but within a few years he admitted that he had lost his passion for the industry. At age 52, he considered it high risk to change careers. I convinced him to test the market. Within less than one year, he accepted the role of CFO for a large hospital. He has never looked back. While balancing a demanding full-time role, he consistently carved out time to explore his options. He faced his fears—that he could fail in the new job and industry at a time when he was funding retirement and children's education. He did not fail and he concurs that by facing his fears and limiting beliefs, he is living a much more fulfilling personal and professional life.

The biggest impediment to becoming a leader is fear. A lack of confidence in one's own abilities causes leaders to play small. The limiting belief that one does not have the resources to handle a crisis or unanticipated results of one's choices leaves leaders standing at the edge of the stage rather than stepping into the limelight. When dealing with an unexpected crisis, no hero or heroine leader was certain that they were taking all the appropriate actions. Armed with the insights gained from this chapter, you can hold center stage during times of crisis, change, and with confidence as you lead yourself and others.

CHAPTER 9

Traits of the New Giants

I have had really good CEOs; CEOs who were even better than I was. They have just enough ego. Confidence and ego—you need that. It passes on and you don't realize it. It's like raising your kids. They watch your movements and subtle things you do, in situations that become a teaching moment. "I want milk in my tea because that's how you do it dad," and you didn't even know he was watching. And suddenly it has become learning lessons unbeknownst to you. [Your behavior] passes down, in turn, to the management group. When you see most people working in their sandboxes and thinking and they are coming up with ideas, all you have to do is manage that. The worst thing is for everyone to look to the CEO [thinking] he/she has all the ideas because the CEO does not. If you get all these other people thinking, it's really magic. You arrive in the office and think, "what are they going to come up with, what are the ideas today?" [The best ideas are] so far out we would never have thought of them. Whatever the culture, whatever is happening, you want your people to never be afraid to talk or afraid to come in with crazy ideas or to come to your office and [make a] pitch.

—Randy Findlay

The business world encountered seismic shifts in advance of the surprise Brexit vote or Donald Trump's presidential election. The US middle class started to shrink at the beginning of the 21st century. In prior decades, the reduction in middle class resulted from an increase in wages and thus prosperity. After 2000, the decline in the middle class resulted from a reduction in earnings across the United States.

For decades, economists have predicted the labor gap that would result when the giant demographic of baby boomers reached retirement age. The common adage of freedom 55 suggested that this shift could start around 2005. This migration of sorts was delayed as North American life expectances are longer, people are more vital, and the baby boomers were and are a generation whose identities are often closely correlated with their work. Many of them were in no hurry to retire. The 2008 global financial crisis decimated retirement savings and confidence for a number of people and contributed to a further delay in the retirement exodus. That has since changed. The shift is now happening. By 2017, as Canada celebrated its 150th birthday, there were more Canadians aged 65 or over than under age 65. The United States faces a similar situation.

In Europe, unemployment varies widely. In 2017, unemployment in Italy is −12 percent and −34 percent for those under 25 years of age. At the same time in the United Kingdom, unemployment is at 2 percent but wages are falling, largely attributed to migrant workers who continue to flow into England. These seismic shifts (and others) have contributed to growing nationalism and protectionist policies across the globe. At the same time, companies of all sizes rely on the global or at least multinational markets in which to sell their products and services. The 360 degree CEO demonstrates some or all of the following six traits in response to or in many cases, in spite of, this changing marketplace with an unpredictable future: ability to lead from summit or basecamp, embrace and leverage diversity, sustained commitment to talent management and succession planning, embracing technological disruption, unwavering commitment to values and knowing "when to go."

Ability to Lead from Summit or Basecamp

A skilled leader stands at the summit and inspires others to traverse what may be a treacherous path to join him or her. He or she identifies the obstacles that may be encountered along the trail while providing encouragement and a sense of urgency. If you are fortunate, you have worked for one of these leaders. Visionary CEOs include Vittorio Colao, CEO of UK Based Vodafone, Randall Stephenson, CEO of AT&T, and Paul Polman, CEO of Unilever.

CEOs who can lead from the basecamp retain an understanding and appreciation of the dynamics at the frontline of the organization. They stay attuned to the customer experience.

At Amazon, CEO Jeff Bezos frequently requests that a chair be left empty at meetings to represent the voice of the customer. Amazon captures an extensive amount of data and fosters innovation by encouraging frontline staff to experiment with changes to shopping carts, and so on.

Zara is a Spanish retailer who gathers both qualitative and quantitative data from their stores on a daily basis. Store staff is expected to converse with customers and seek out their opinions on how products could be improved. Zara attributes this regular and ongoing data gathering to bottom line results; their failed product introductions are almost 9 percent less than the industry average and they produce nearly 10 times as much product as their largest competitors.

Ed Clark, former CEO of TD Bank Financial Group, is a visionary leader who demonstrated the ability to lead from the summit and basecamp. While Ed was CEO of TD Bank, he could sometimes be found in TD Canada Trust branches a distance away from Bay Street. While vacationing at his cottage he might step into the local branch in shorts and a t-shirt. Following the TD Canada Trust merger, Ed was occasionally spotted walking the line in one of the retail branches, introducing himself to customers and tellers working the front line. When leading from basecamp as well as from the summit, Ed, Jeff Bezos, and Amancio Ortega contribute positively to the bottom line. This is evident in their sustained financial performance. Their actions and practices contribute to policies that empower and motivate employees throughout the organization. Their behavior contributes to the folklore and storytelling that is a hallmark of organizations with a strong culture. Customer service is favorably impacted.

Now it's your turn.

Exercise #10—What is your elevation? Basecamp, summit, or on the climb?
Are you leading from both the summit and basecamp? Consider the following. Ask members of your team. It can be interesting to discover where your perceptions are aligned and where they differ.

Summit

- Do you have a clearly articulated vision and purpose? Can your employees explain why the company exists and describe what it looks like when you are meeting your vision?
- Would your board agree that you are successfully executing on your strategy?
- Do you effectively balance short-term goals with a commitment to the long-term success of the company, for example, make appropriate capital investments that may impact immediate and short-term financial results but will position the company for long-term success?
- Do your employees hear from you at least four times per year—in a town hall, on video, on-site visits?

Basecamp

- Do you capture current data from the front line that reflects the customer experience?
- If you have data, are you using it to reward great performance, to promptly address poor performance, or to remove obstacles that inhibit frontline employees or frustrate customers?
  - I have seen many companies using the data to set sales targets at the store, regional, and national level. That is insufficient and when ineffectively applied, simply demotivates some of your best sales people.
- If you conduct an employee engagement survey, do you take action every year in response to employee feedback? If not, and if you cannot commit to doing so, stop conducting the survey; it is doing you more harm than good. Or, better yet, start to heed the feedback and take committed action every year.

Embrace and Leverage Diversity

A popular 1984 advertisement read, "Everybody is united by the Colors of Benneton. No matter your race, color or sex." This organization has continued to promote diversity through publicizing often-controversial photographs in an enduring aspiration to promote peace and acceptance. Their courage of conviction is consistent with the second trait of the new giants of leadership.

Some CEOs do not regard the promotion of diversity as a courageous act. However, too many still do. Diversity does not simply apply to ethnicity or gender as in the Benneton slogan but also to diversity of: thought and expressed opinion, age, sexual orientation, religion, dress, background, experience, communication style, and so on.

> We specifically look for diversity because diversity is what gives you better solutions. I don't need you to think like me; that is not helpful. It is helpful if you have a diverse experience, skills, philosophy, etc. That is how you solve the most complex business problems.
>
> —Suzanne West

> How I go about creating [diversity]? It starts with the values set and respect for all people. I try to always model that. It's everything from knowing the name of the security guard and telling them hello or you know the person who cleans the washroom. I tell them hello in the same way I tell an executive or a peer. I think people see that. And it starts with a fundamental respect and I just try to demonstrate that.
>
> I actually try very hard to move beyond the visible minority element. I think we have a way to go even on that. What I'm trying to do here is uncover [our] biases that are part of the processes of the selection; I think that is where diversity starts in an organization. Having visibly diverse style and thinking goes all the way back to ensuring that we don't have these subtle

biases that screen people out before they even get in the door or before they even get through a process.

—Gianna Manes

It is not enough to simply mobilize a group of people with varied backgrounds and experiences. As a leader, you need to ensure that your management team and employees learn how to respect, honor, and harness the benefits of diversity. This can be achieved through training programs as well as through you demonstrating the best leadership behavior.

- Encourage debate at the executive table.
- Reach into the organization and seek out opinions of newer employees or those in customer-facing roles.
- Explicitly ask others (at all levels and in every department) to challenge the status quo, to kill a few proverbial sacred cows.
- Recognize those on your management team who enable debate among their staff, who promote new ideas and who will change their position or point of view when presented with data and a valid opposing position.

We provide [all of our employees with training] to function well with diversity. We try to get people to the place where they are seeking out different [points of view], e.g. "This is my proposal. I want you to read it and tell me what is wrong with it." [We want people to ask, "What is the best thing [option or decision] for the greatest good?"] That is how you harness the power of diversity without creating all the madness the world is trying to do in dividing [people].

—Suzanne West

The following is evidence of the progress yet to be made on diversity: the continuing dialogue on how to "manage millennials" at the same time that seasoned professionals in Fortune 500 companies are complaining that they are experiencing ageism, the US travel ban for those from predominantly Muslim countries, the representation of women on corporate boards in North America (the numbers are better in Europe), even the black, gray, and blue suits that predominate Wall Street. If you consider the last item to be weak evidence of a lack of diversity, contrast this with business meetings in Mumbai or Delhi where executive women in positions with considerable responsibility may be dressed in saris while conducting business. Their feminine dress does not detract from their reputation or impact if they are intelligent, collaborative, capable leaders.

Leveraging diversity is not about altruism or corporate social responsibility. It is a wise financial decision. Companies that encourage diversity of thought, who foster debate, which employ professionals with a breadth of functional and social experiences, enjoy better customer relationships, lower employee turnover, and greater profitability. Some of the US companies that have been recognized for employing a diverse workforce include: Aetna, Aramark Corp., Burger King, FedEx, Marriott, Starwood Hotels, and McDonalds.

Creating diversity in the organization should not be delegated to Human Resources or Corporate Services. The responsibility starts with the CEO and the board. The executive of TransCanada was fairly homogeneous. The directors of the TransCanada board asked management to prioritize addressing this imbalance and they have made active strides in doing so. This cannot be addressed in a single year and requires a sustained commitment to talent management and succession planning—the third trait of the new giants.

Sustained Talent Management and Succession Planning

Successful CEOs and business owners know that deferred succession planning creates gaps in leadership and typically takes three to five years to resolve. Some Fortune 500 companies run hot and cold on their talent management processes. They hire consultants and/or charge their HR group with implementing professional development plans, with identifying high potential performers and mentoring. Then when the economy weakens or their industry struggles, when financial performance is lacking or EBITA takes a hit, they retreat in their actions. Sometimes the rationale is that there are more talented professionals than there are jobs, that culling of positions means fewer executive roles, that professional development is discretionary and therefore can and should be deferred until a period of greater prosperity or low candidate supply.

360 degree CEOs consider succession and talent management to be an all-weather strategic priority. Talent management is on the agenda at board meetings at least once per year. The executives and middle management assess and review the pool of internal talent once or twice each year, regardless of economic cycle or the company's financial results. Every leader has responsibility to support the development of their best employees. In Fortune 500 companies, CEOs, on average, have more than 15 years of tenure with the company before being appointed to the top job. In small- and mid-sized companies, once a potential successor is identified, a successful transition most often requires three to five years of mentoring and development. For this reason alone, when companies defer talent management as a priority for a period of time, there is always a lag when the topic returns to the forefront.

Fortune Magazine recognized IBM, Unilever, Deere, and McKinsey for grooming talent. IBM sends leadership SWAT teams to locations across the globe. Young executives at Unilever spend time in small villages in order to better understand the needs of impoverished customers in rural India and John Deere board directors provide coaching to high potential managers.

It's Not All About Retention

The best leaders do not limit talent development to grooming high potentials and creating opportunities. Successful companies expect leaders to identify those who are no longer a fit, who are disengaged, or who may be blocking developmental opportunities for others. When Jack Welch led GE, they infamously identified the "bottom 10%" every year and exited people from the company. At TD Bank, when executives met to provide updates on the development plans for high potentials, there was an expectation that leaders identified those who had become "blockers" or were not meeting performance expectations. As with high potential candidates, executives were expected to provide development opportunities but it was clearly recognized that one must make decisions that were in the best interest of the company over time. As markets, companies, and customers change, CEOs must proactively evaluate and sometimes alter their workforce.

> We are trying to create unique and exciting lives for people. Those who embrace that and want to contribute, to be on the team and are prepared to be engaged… if they have a moment of weakness, we'll pick them up and we'll carry them along with us on that journey. But I've also said to employees, "those of you that are disengaged, not interested, or can't be bothered to get interested, let us help you find some place where you'll be engaged, invited and successful because it's not going to be here. Don't spend every day going to do something that you're not excited about."
>
> —Mayo Schmidt

Sharon Ludlow has a passion for developing talent and mentoring leaders.

> For me the most important part of my role is being able to provide a vision and then empowering people to achieve it. The best part of my job is watching people learn and grow and then succeed. I deliberately hired people that were smarter than I was in certain topic areas. I can draw the long-term vision and they can provide the complementary 'how do I get there' skills. It was always really important to see people grow and to provide that empowerment.
>
> —Sharon Ludlow

The advice that I have given repeatedly, as I had learned it, is that all staff at all levels should think of their career not as a vertical ladder but as a lattice ladder. Lattice—just as you would see it on the top of a fence. Ultimately, you may find yourself at a very senior level, but your path may have taken you laterally; or diagonally; and in some roles you may even have had to step back. I know people hesitate to consider roles that aren't an obvious promotion, but if an opportunity offers you more breadth of experience and a different path, I am always a big advocate. When succession planning for my direct reports and for theirs, I would intentionally say, "We're not going to talk about how you get to the next rung on the ladder. We're going to talk about your skills and capabilities." Often, employees simply say "I want that job, title X." I always say, "forget title X," or "forget compensation," at least to a certain degree. Tell me what you want to do. Are you the person who was always the schoolteacher in hiding, at your best when you're teaching or coaching others? If that's the case, rather than you moving to a technical role, maybe you are better in coaching mode on a project team where you're training people on new initiatives, versus someone who's at his/her desk doing the mathematical calculations behind an insurance deal."

"I encourage people to always think of it as the lattice and then change the frame of the discussion entirely away from, 'How do you get to the next level?' to 'How do you gain a broader skill set?' It was pretty helpful. Where it gets a little challenging is at the level right below the CEO role where they may have made some lattice moves in their career. That gets a bit more challenging because those individuals are saying, 'I've been there and done that and after 25 years I'm ready to move up.

—Sharon Ludlow

If that is not sufficient rationale to support a commitment to talent management, consider the demographic reality. Economists have been predicting a labor shortage for decades. The first baby boomers are well past 65. The 2008 global financial crisis delayed retirements and the now common transition to part time and self-employment in one's 60s. But now it is real. While a higher percentage of 65+ Americans are working than ever before, they are working less and many have retired. In Canada, the majority of the population is 65 or over.

Embracing Technological Disruption

In 1930, British economist Keynes predicted a 15-hour workweek by 2030. While Europeans typically work fewer hours than North Americans, Nicolas Sarkozy of France eliminated the 35-hour workweek several years ago and for working Europeans, the workweek may be moving closer to North American norms. However, technology has and will continue to disrupt the employment picture.

When the price of oil dropped from its all-time high of over US$147 per barrel to the $30 per barrel range, producers dramatically reduced their operating costs. While some companies went out of business, many were able to sustain margins at $35 and $40 per barrel. We have all seen the reduction in jobs in North America in automotive, mining, and manufacturing. Robotics and labor arbitrage through offshoring have changed the employment picture in manufacturing. The service industry is the biggest employment category across the world. Walmart employs over 2 million people. Amazon employs 200,000. What will happen to jobs in retail stores such as Walmart when more consumers opt for Amazon-like services? It is possible that the combination of a smaller labor pool and automation will increase unemployment. However, the aging population will require many support services such as healthcare, retrofit housing, mobility aids, burial services, and more. And steadily increasing population growth, primarily in developing countries, will place demands on access to goods and services.

The implications are that companies must consistently reinvent themselves, not always through radical change but through continuous improvement through innovation and process improvement. This has always and remains best achieved through engaging the hearts and minds of your employees and actively soliciting their feedback and ideas. In Hal Kvisle's words, "leadership is not thinking about what is our next great idea but rather, what do I have to do to stimulate and empower this group of people to think up some really good ideas and then how do I encourage them to get it on the right track?"

He shared his view that the key obligation of a CEO is to first ensure that there are good ideas coming up and being debated, discussed, and refined and, as importantly, to ensure that the rigor of a good decision quality process is applied to every decision.

Unwavering Commitment to Values

As you become more senior in an organization you are faced with issues that test your values. There's an old saying that God invented writing to show us how messy our thinking is; well I think that the issues faced by an Executive manager are simply tests that show us how messy our understanding is of our personal values. Difficult issues, and the subsequent decisions, help you refine and more clearly articulate what your values mean to you. For example, everyone has a value of integrity, but what does that really mean? It's not until you get severely tested that you begin to more fully develop what that means to you. Some would say well that's just rationalizing, but I view it as finding a better definition, a brighter clarity as to what your values are in those testing situations.

—Cal Yonker

As leaders, we are faced every day with decisions that you do need to use your values and ethics to be able to come to an answer. I distil it down to doing the right thing. As I look back in my career, I am most proud of coming out of Viterra that there was never ever an incident in 12 years and 7,000 people that anyone embarrassed the organization by demonstrating a lack of adherence to values and judgments and ethics. I travelled from office to office, first safety then values and ethics.

One person in a faraway place that no one even knows could do something that puts at risk or peril the reputation and the people in the organization. I am happy and most proud that we navigated all those years and complex decisions and, our business being global, we were dealing with managing around countries that had sanctions, governments that were not behaving in a way that was acceptable to the countries in which we operated and we had to manage. I think you are called on all the time to make decisions and you have to reach down and say "what do my values tell me is the right thing to do here?" I don't think I have ever been tempted to violate my values. There is nothing that I want that is so valuable to create a circumstance when I would even consider it. There is not a prize great enough to ask me to do something that I can't stand up with my head high and say I did the right thing.

—Mayo Schmidt

The above examples demonstrate how 360 degree CEOs stay aligned to their personal values. Colleen Abdoulah's example below describes how she ensured that her values were operationalized throughout an organization.

Culture was our key differentiator. I spoke [about it] to all 600 employees. "We're the David of David and Goliath. Our competitors can outspend us and out price us. Our costs are 30 percent higher than theirs. They can always have more R&D; they can spend money on capital and research. So how do we compete? We have to create a differentiator. It's not going to be our products and it's not going to be our price. And the only thing I know that cannot be duplicated is us. How we think, how we feel, how we interact, how we make our customers feel and how we interact with them. We're going to create a culture centered on the differentiation of us. How we do it will be a differentiator, not what we do. Because the "what" can be commoditized, it can be duplicated all day long. But the "how" cannot."

We created a purpose statement. We created our values and we operationalized our values. We recruited, trained, hired or developed people [in alignment with our values]. We incorporated it into their merit increases and promoted people based on how they modeled our values. And if you purposely violated one, we had zero tolerance and you would be dismissed immediately.

When we first rolled it out we had maybe two instances across the company where that happened and it didn't happen again. People knew that we meant zero tolerance. So we operationalized being rebellious, having a clear purpose statement about why we exist, stating that how matters more than what. And having what we call the service structure.

Structure your whole organization first around defining the needs and expectations of your external customers down to a very fine point. Then build your internal customers' processes around meeting those needs and expectations. So the silos that are traditional in a hierarchical culture and environment are blown away. You identify who your primary internal customer is. For us that was the front line because they had the direct contact with the customer and in cable they were the lowest people on the rung. They were after-thoughts. They were told what to do. In our environment, our culture, they were the primary customers. So when they said we need X, Y, Z on our trucks, we need this kind of data at the call center, we had to do it. That turned everything on its head.

In those days, you had to wait a day for the cable guy. Maybe if you were lucky they give you a morning or an afternoon. But that was four hours people were sitting around for the cable guy. We were there in an hour, at maximum two hours. That's how we differentiated ourselves and we won. When I left, [WOW had received] 19 first place J.D. Power awards for customer excellence. No one in our industry has ever done that before or since. [In your book *Feet to the Fire,* you write about accountability] and for me, that's key. In our culture, everybody felt a level of ownership and pride and accountability because they knew who their internal customers were. There was no infighting, there was no backstabbing or bureaucracy or politics. Everybody cared about getting it done right. The level of accountability was so high. And you have to support that financially. In private equity we were given 10 percent of equity to distribute. Traditionally the CEO usually gets 25 percent of the 10 percent. I took 13 percent and gave the rest to the team. Much of the team had equity right down to the supervisors in the field. It was a small amount but it was a lot for them. I also said, culturally, that there would never be a bonus given out, or a merit increase for management unless everybody got one. Too often I saw senior people getting merits or getting bonuses when no one else did. I always thought that was wrong. People knew that neither me, nor management were going to get bonuses unless everybody did. If the company did well, everybody did well and that increased the level of accountability.

Also what increased the recovery [of the business] was transparency. They saw all the numbers, so that they could understand all the costs. Technicians who had been in the business for 15 years had no idea what it cost to outfit a truck. Now they knew. They had no idea what their tools cost. Now they knew down to the tool level that if they wasted equipment and wasted materials that was going to cost them their bonus. I would be in a coffee room at one of our locations and I'd hear a technician go up and go, "Frank, you know, you were at XXX last month and you didn't change the splitter out. Now I have to go back there and it costs $150 in a repeat truck roll."

That's music to CEO's ears, right? For them to care about every repeat truck roll because they knew we would tell them every month how many repeats were unnecessary and what that cost us and as a result, cost them. In an industry that is not known for employee satisfaction or customer satisfaction, ours received a 94.2 percent satisfaction rating from our customers and 97.3 from our employees. I am most proud of that.

—Colleen Abdoulah

Knowing When to Go

In the words of Kenny Rogers, "You got to know when to hold 'em and know when to fold 'em, know when to walk away and know when to run." One of my highly successful clients is 61 years old and has been in the top position at her publicly traded company for almost 10 years. While she has not yet set a date to depart, we have discussed that inevitable point in the future. In her 50s, she promised herself that once she turned 60, she would check in with herself at least once per year and ask, "Am I still having fun? Am I still adding value? Am I blocking others from bringing new and better ideas to the leadership of the company? Am I still meeting the expectations of the board?" As soon as she finds herself saying no to one or more of these questions and/or when her judgment tells her it is time to retire, she will take that step. She has two potential heirs-apparent and capable successors. When she announces her departure, it is expected that there will be a smooth transition; she exhibits the third trait noted previously, she sponsors a robust succession-planning program at her company.

The most self-aware leaders have the humility and healthy self-esteem to step away when the indicators suggest they should do so. This could be advice from a spouse, a health issue, disagreements with the board, lack of interest and excitement about the role, when the leader believes that they have taken the company where they wanted to and perhaps as far as they can and it is ready for a fresh view and new leadership. These transitions are not always retirement, but can be a sabbatical or a move to a new leadership role. Some CEOs make moves on a regular basis. They may do so to engage in new challenges, to run a larger company, to work in a new industry, or because they are turnaround CEOs who prefer to depart when operations are stable. Whatever the reason, CEOs seek authority, autonomy, variety, and an intellectual challenge.

Let's consider some well-known CEO transitions. Bill Gates handed over the CEO reins at Microsoft in 2000. The Bill and Melinda Gates Foundation was founded the same year, and, in 2006, Gates turned his full attention to the foundation. While **he found a new passion,** it was consistent with the business of Microsoft; he leverages technology to benefit others.

Sam Walton retired at age 70 and handed the reins over to his protégé, a long-time Walmart leader, David Glass. Between Walton's retirement in 1988 and his death in 1992, Walmart had unprecedented growth becoming the largest retailer in the United States. Today it is the third largest employer in the world, employing over 2 million people. Sam Walton **recognized that it was time for someone else to run the company.**

In 2014, Larry Ellison announced that he would step down as Oracle's CEO and become CTO and executive chair. As CTO, Ellis is **returning to his original interest** while maintaining a path of acquisition. Like Sam Walton, Bill Gates and the CEO I described previously, Ellison had two capable and ready successors. Mark Hurd and Safra Catz now share the CEO role.

There are a variety of factors that influence the timing of a CEO stepping aside. As noted earlier, they can include: finding a new passion, knowing that new leadership is in the best interest of the company, returning to the roots of your interests, or for personal reasons such as family, health, or the need for a new challenge. Whatever the reason, the differentiator of the 360 degree CEO is that he/she accepts or identifies when a change is appropriate and does not overstay their welcome.

Conclusion

360 degree CEOs and executives are all around us. They are leading small enterprises, mid-cap firms, and global behemoths. One need not look that far to find them. They are trying, failing, learning, and trying again. They care about their employees and their customers. They are passionate about making a difference and they live in alignment with the values they espouse. They are generating profits and stimulating our economies, providing jobs and much-needed products and services. This book provides you the opportunity to hear from them directly. Take the lessons and ideas that are relevant for you and apply them to your leadership practice—whatever level you are in the organization. And when the media, your colleagues, politicians, or your own experiences indicate a dearth of leaders today, point to these fine examples, and the many others that are making a meaningful contribution every day.

I think the lack of personal time or the lack of being present as being one of the penalties of leadership. This leads to self-sacrifice and that needs to be balanced because it can't be all one way or the other. I think most of life is balance and trying to maintain that unique balance. I think about this all the time.

—Mayo Schmidt

We serve with heart. We lead with courage. And we celebrate with grace.

—Colleen Abdoulah

On the really big stuff. I don't start with "what people will say?" I start with, "what really does matter?" It's the mirror test. What I am going to look in the mirror tomorrow and feel proud of?

—Gianna Manes

At Canada Trust [prior to merger with TD] in 1994, we were providing same sex benefits before most companies and before all governments. In 2002, I was quite shocked [to learn that few were taking the benefits and that] I was running a homophobic organization that made people uncomfortable to ask for their basic rights as an employee. I underestimated the opposition. I was a bit naïve. I had to make this a personal CEO objective and this was not going away. I had to get out and campaign and keep on campaigning and I would probably keep on campaigning to this very day. We are not going to let up. "No. At TD we are going to do the right thing. And we are going to do the right thing for 10 or 15 years from now."

—Ed Clark

In terms of legacy, I guess what I always felt once I get into it a little more that if I had to leave a legacy it would be to leave the company in a better position than it was when I assumed the role. And I think that probably came true.

—Brian MacNeill

The role of CEO of this company is about understanding where are the areas that we do need to evolve and become better. Understanding how that drives value to our customers and how that differentiates what we do from our competitors. That's the general role innovation plays in our company…

There are heroes out there. I see them all the time. It's where you turn your eyes to, what you're watching. If you watch the news, sure there's bad guys. But look around you; there are heroes all round.

—Cal Yonker

I am just more interested in being extraordinary than in failing. Failure is just as important as other things in trying and you have to get to the brink twice to know what your potential is.

—Suzanne West

APPENDIX

The 360 Degree CEOs

Sharon M. Ludlow, CPA, CA, ICD.D
Former President & CEO, Swiss Re Canada

Sharon is a C-suite executive, uniquely positioned with more than 25 years of experience in both the Life & Health and Property & Casualty (P&C) insurance industries. She served as President & CEO, Swiss Re Canada, one of the world's largest reinsurers; and President, Aviva Insurance Company of Canada, Canada's 2nd largest P&C insurer.

Currently, Sharon is Head, Insurance Investment Strategy at OMERS, one of Canada's largest defined benefit pension plans. In this role, Sharon is responsible for setting and executing the strategic plan with respect to OMERS insurance investments.

During her tenure in the life insurance industry, Sharon played a key role in the demutualization and IPO of Canada Life Financial (now owned by Great West Life). In 2000, along with co-founders, Sharon launched Kanetix, Canada's first on-line insurance marketplace for consumers.

Sharon is a Chartered Accountant/Chartered Professional Accountant. She holds a Bachelor of Commerce degree from the University of Toronto and earned her CA designation in 1992. Sharon is a graduate of the Directors Education Program, Rotman School of Management and holds an ICD.D (Institute of Corporate Directors) designation. Sharon also holds an FLMI (Fellow, Life Management Institute) designation.

Sharon has extensive experience serving in the insurance industry as Director of the Board for Green Shield Canada (2016-present), the Insurance Bureau of Canada (2012–2016); Canadian Life & Health Insurance Association (2012–2014); Institute for Catastrophic Loss Reduction (2010–2016); and Reinsurance Research Council (2010–2014).

In 2013, Sharon was named by WXN one of Canada's Top 100 Most Powerful Women; and one of the Top 50 Women in the insurance industry globally by Reactions magazine.

Sharon has actively volunteered for Junior Achievement of Canada and has held Treasurer and President and Chair of the Board positions for various non-profit organizations.

Paul Kelly
CEO, Connect First Credit Union

Paul is currently the CEO of Connect First Credit Union. Paul has been with Connect First and its predecessor First Calgary since 1995, joining the credit union as the Chief Financial Officer. Connect First was founded almost 80 years ago and is Canada's 10th largest credit union, with 100,000 members and $5 billion in assets under administration. Paul holds an HBA from Western University as well as an MBA from York University. Prior to joining the Canadian credit union system, Paul worked in the trust and electrical utility industries in finance roles. Paul is an active participant in credit union system governance; he sits on the board of Alberta Central as well as the board of the Canadian Credit Union Association. Active in the nonprofit sector, Paul is a board member of the Canadian Mental Health Association as well as the Safe Haven Foundation. In 2012, Paul received the ICD.D designation.

Mayo Schmidt
President and CEO of Hydro One Limited and Hydro One Inc.

Mr. Mayo Schmidt is the President and Chief Executive Officer of Hydro One. Prior to joining Hydro One, Mr. Schmidt served as President, Chief Executive Officer, at Viterra, Inc., a global food ingredients company operating in 14 countries. Early in his career, Mr. Schmidt held a number of key management positions of increasing responsibility at General Mills, Inc. until he joined ConAgra as President of their Canadian operations and spearheaded ConAgra's expansion into Canada. In 2007, he led a $2.0 billion acquisition of Agricore United, then a $2.2 billion acquisition of ABB, Australia's leading agriculture corporation, growing Viterra, Inc. from a $200 million Market Cap to finally a sale in 2012 for over $7.5 billion. Mr. Schmidt currently sits on the Board of Directors of Agrium Inc. as Chairman of the Governance Committee and Chairman of the Special Committee for the Merger of Equals of Agrium and Potash Corp. forming a $38 billion global fertilizer giant. He is a member of Harvard

University Private and Public, Scientific, Academic, and Consumer Food Policy Group, and is on Washburn University's Foundation board of Trustees. Mr. Schmidt received his Honorary Doctorate of Commerce from Washburn in 2016 and his BBA from Washburn in 1980.

Suzanne West
President and CEO of Imaginea Energy

She is the President and CEO of Imaginea Energy. A fearless leader. A visionary.

She is going to change the world. And she's going to do it by getting other people to change the world with her. Imaginea is her latest venture and one of five companies that, over the past 15 years, she has successfully built from scratch. She spent her early days receiving an engineering degree from the University of Calgary, then spent the first 11 years of her career as a reservoir engineer and in various leadership positions in large corporations.

Her unparalleled wisdom, that only a brilliant and successful entrepreneur can offer, has attracted a crack team to break down the most daunting of barriers. To rewire the way we think about energy. To turn what we're doing into what we should be doing. Her latest passion, Imaginea, is to create a new type of energy company that values all three of planet, people, and profits equally. Essentially, to discover a better way of developing our resources and creating "AND" solutions and new possibilities to transform the energy industry into a force for good. Her truly laudable career has crystallized into an epiphany—that profits are not the nemesis of this planet and the people on it. That oil doesn't have to be a dirty word. That change can happen, and it will happen because it's the smartest thing to do.

And it's this vision, guided by her insight and astonishing ambitions, that unites our ranks and compels us to realize our great potential.

Gianna Manes
President and CEO, ENMAX Corporation

Gianna Manes, President and CEO of ENMAX Corporation, has nearly three decades of experience in the energy industry. She spent the first part of her career in the gas pipeline business in Houston, Texas, before transitioning to the electricity industry. Gianna has experience in a number of electricity markets across the United States, Europe, and Alberta, Canada.

Before joining ENMAX in Calgary in 2012 as President and CEO, Gianna served as the Senior Vice President and Chief Customer Officer for Duke Energy, a large North American power company based in Charlotte, North Carolina.

Born and raised in Louisiana, Gianna earned a Bachelor of Science degree in industrial engineering from Louisiana State University, a Master of Business Administration degree from the University of Houston, and completed the Harvard Business School Advanced Management Program.

Gianna currently serves as a member of the board of directors for Keyera Corp., the Canadian Electricity Association and the Energy Council of Canada. She also holds the ICD.D designation from the Rotman School of Management. In 2014, she served as Co-Chair of the Calgary and Area United Way campaign, and was elected to the United Way of Calgary and Area Board of Directors in 2015.

Gianna has been recognized for her leadership and accomplishments throughout her career: as Electricity Human Resources Canada's CEO of the Year in 2013, one of Alberta Venture's Top 50 Most Influential People in 2015, and one of Canada's Most Powerful Women by the Women's Executive Network.

Colleen Abdoulah
Former CEO/Chair, WOW! Internet, Cable, and Phone

Colleen Abdoulah is the only female CEO to have led a top-10 cable operating company. Raised by parents who emphasized empathy and respect for all, her leadership style and personal commitment to serving others is widely known and respected and is reflected in her passionate focus on customer experience and company culture.

Colleen guided WOW! Internet, Cable, and Phone for 12 years, overseeing industry-leading financial success and creating unprecedented value for employees and shareholders. During her tenure, WOW! quadrupled its customer base from 200,000+ to more than 800,000, growing revenues to more than $1.2 billion. Under Colleen's leadership, WOW! earned a remarkable 19 J.D. Power and Associates awards for customer satisfaction, multiple top-provider awards from Consumer Reports, and the PC Magazine Readers' Choice Award for top cable Internet service provider. She is equally proud of the many awards WOW! received as an employer, including recognition as a 2012 and 2013 National Best and Brightest Companies to Work For winner.

Prior to joining WOW!, Colleen spent much of her career at Tele-Communications Inc. (TCI), where she served in a number of positions including Assistant COO and Executive Vice President of Cable Operations. Her professional career spans over 30 years in the marketing/advertising and telecommunications industries.

She is Former Chair of the Board of the American Cable Association, a lobbying organization representing the interests of independent cable operators. She also served on the board of C-SPAN, and is a former Vice President of the Executive Board of Women in Cable and Telecommunications, as well as Former Chairperson for the WICT Foundation.

In the nonprofit world, Colleen is an ardent voice and advocate for those who have been marginalized. She is a former Chair of the Board for the Rocky Mountain Children's Law Center, and she currently serves on the boards of the Women's College of the University of Denver; the Women's Forum of Colorado; and is Chair of World Pulse, a global social network dedicated to connecting, uniting, and empowering women around the world. She also currently serves on the board of Rocky Mountain PBS and is an industry advisor for Avista Capital Partners in New York.

As keynote speaker at a variety of management conferences and business forums, Colleen has shared her views on the strategic importance of customer experience and company culture; development of gender-balanced management and leadership; and cultivation of authentic leadership, among other topics.

Colleen graduated from Mount Royal University in Calgary, Alberta, and received her MBA from the University of Denver. She is the recipient of numerous honors and awards, including the Leaders Advancing and Helping Communities (LAHC) Lifetime Achievement Award; the Colorado Women's Chamber of Commerce Top 25 Most Powerful Women Award; the American Cable Association's PAC Individual Leadership Award; and was a Multichannel News Wonder Women honoree and an inductee to the WICT Rocky Mountain Chapter's Walk of Fame.

Luc Desjardins
President and CEO, Superior Plus

Mr. Desjardins is President and Chief Executive Officer of Superior Plus Corp., a public company based in Toronto, Ontario, that provides propane distribution and marketing services, and specialty chemical production. Mr. Desjardins is also an independent Director of Canadian Imperial Bank of Commerce, since February 2009. Prior to joining Superior Plus in 2011, Mr. Desjardins was a partner of the Sterling Group LLP, a private equity firm located in Houston, Texas. Mr. Desjardins also served as President and Chief Executive Officer at Transcontinental Inc., third largest printer in North America and largest in Mexico, from 2004 to 2008 and Chief Operating Officer from 2000 to 2004. Mr. Desjardins holds a Masters of Business Administration degree from the University of Quebec and is a graduate of the Harvard Business School Management Development Program.

Brian F. MacNeill
Former President and CEO, Enbridge Inc.

Mr. MacNeill retired as President and CEO of Enbridge Inc. on January 2001. Prior thereto he was CEO and Director of Enbridge from 1990 to 2001 and previously served as Chair of PetroCanada and Dofasco Inc. He also had board positions with TD Bank, Telus Inc., Sears Canada, Capital Power Corp, and Veritas DGC Inc.

Mr. MacNeill was appointed as a Member of the Order of Canada. In addition, he received the CEO award of the year from the University of Calgary School of Business and CEO of the Year Award from the University of Alberta School of Business and is a member of the Petroleum Hall of Fame.

Geoffrey C. Pulford CPA, CA
Consulting

Geoff's professional focus has been primarily on small and medium-size businesses. He followed his CA designation with several years at Bank of Montreal. Armed with a strong financial foundation from a decade of public accounting and commercial banking, Geoff took over the reins of a small medical business that was close to bankruptcy. Within eight years he had turned the nearly bankrupt company around, grown it, made it profitable, and sold it—earning shareholders a substantial return on their original investment. Geoff remained with the acquiring company, Airgas Inc., a NYSE listed company based in Philadelphia. As a subsidiary president he oversaw a period of explosive growth as the company expanded from medical gases to industrial gases opening 17 new stores in the first year. From Airgas he became CEO of a midsize regional law firm—Harrison Pensa LLP, where he spent 17 years. Geoff's tenure as CEO coincided with the early stages of the full-scale transformation of the legal marketplace. This transformation created new opportunities for lawyers to better serve their clients—but it also created new demands and higher pressures to deliver better value to the market. Recognizing that law firms needed to dedicate themselves to client-focused innovation, Geoff guided Harrison Pensa into a leadership position in this area. Under Geoff's direction, Harrison Pensa developed numerous innovations, most notably a proprietary debt collection system employed by insurance and financial institutions across Canada. Administered by paralegals and law clerks, lawyer involvement is minimal, thanks to its LEAN operating principles and a high utilization of technology. He will tell you that there is much more to do in the legal services area.

In 2014, he left his position at Harrison Pensa and started a consulting practice advising business owners on exit transitions. That practice led him and his business partner to purchase a high-end window and door manufacturing company. In addition, and continuing with his progressive views on technology, Geoff is the Chief Operating Officer and Chief Financial Officer of a software startup that provides connected vehicles with a fully autonomous solution for parking and road tolling.

A graduate of Bishop's University in Lennoxville, Quebec, Geoff earned his designation as Chartered Accountant at PricewaterhouseCoopers.

Throughout his career, Geoff has been committed to community service including numerous fundraising campaigns, Boards, and advisory committees. In addition, Geoff volunteers his time to mentor and coach aspiring young business people who are starting their own companies.

Harold (Hal) Kvisle
Board Chair, ARC Resources
Corporate Director; Former CEO of Talisman Energy and Trans-Canada Corporation

Hal Kvisle has served as a leader in the oil and gas, utilities and power generation industries for more than 35 years. He currently serves as board chair of ARC Resources Ltd, and was chief executive officer of Talisman Energy from 2012 to 2015. From 2001 to 2010 Mr. Kvisle was chief executive officer of TransCanada Corporation. Prior to joining TransCanada in 1999 he was the founder and president of Fletcher Challenge Energy Canada, from 1990 to 1999. He held engineering, finance, and management positions with Dome Petroleum Limited from 1975 to 1988. Mr. Kvisle holds a Bachelor of Science in Engineering from the University of Alberta and a Master in Business Administration from the Haskayne School, University of Calgary.

Ed Clark
Former CEO of TD Bank Financial Group

Ed Clark retired as Group President and CEO of TD Bank Group on November 1, 2014 after 12 years as CEO.

Following TD's acquisition of Canada Trust Financial Services in February of 2000, Ed joined TD Bank Group as Chairman and Chief Executive Officer of TD Canada Trust. In this role he oversaw the successful integration of the TD and Canada Trust banking operations. He then served as President and Chief Operating Officer starting in July 2000. Before joining TD, Ed was President and Chief Executive Officer of Canada Trust Financial Services.

In 1985, he joined Merrill Lynch, and three years later Ed was appointed Chairman and Chief Executive Officer of Morgan Financial Corporation, a position he held until he joined Canada Trust Financial Services Inc. in 1991. From 1974 to 1984, Ed held a number of senior positions in the federal government. In 1982, he won the Outstanding Civil Servant of the Year Award.

Ed graduated from the University of Toronto in 1969 with a Bachelor of Arts degree. He earned his Master's degree and Doctorate in Economics from Harvard University in 1971 and 1974 respectively. Ed has also received honorary degrees from Mount Allison University, Queen's University, Western University, University of Toronto, York University, and Ryerson University.

Ed previously served as a Director on the Board of TD Bank Group, and as Chairman of the Board of TD Bank N.A. and its subsidiary banks. He also served as Vice-Chairman of the Board of TD Ameritrade Holding Corporation. He was the 2010 Cabinet Chair for United Way Toronto, and is currently a member of the Chair's Advisory Council for Habitat for Humanity Toronto. He provides support to WoodGreen Community Services, an organization that delivers programs to build sustainable communities in the Toronto area, and to Egale, Canada's only national charity promoting lesbian, gay, bisexual, and trans (LGBT) human rights.

In 2014, Ed was elected to the Board of Trustees of US public policy organization, the Brookings Institute. He was also appointed Chair of the Premier's Advisory Council on Government Assets by Ontario Premier Kathleen Wynne and in 2015, he was appointed Business Advisor to Premier Wynne. Additionally, Ed was named to a housing task force by Toronto Mayor John Tory that is looking into how Toronto Community Housing serves the people of Toronto and how it is governed. Ed was appointed a Director of Thomson Reuters in 2015.

Ed has been recognized in Canada and around the world for his leadership at work and in the community. He was acknowledged by GTA Association of Fundraising Professionals (AFP) with the 2011 Outstanding Philanthropist Award.

Ed is regularly asked to speak at a number of prominent international events on a wide range of topics, including the Canadian economy, the banking industry, leadership values, and the importance of creating a diverse and inclusive culture in the workplace.

Ed has been honored numerous times for his vision, integrity, and strong leadership. He was appointed to the Order of Canada in 2010— one of the country's highest distinctions—for his "contributions to Canada's banking and financial industry, and for his voluntary and philanthropic endeavours." Ed has also received Egale's Leadership Award in honor of his leadership in supporting LGBT communities, and the inaugural Catalyst Canada Honour, awarded to individuals who have made a critical and visible difference to women's advancement.

In 2010, Ed was named Canada's Outstanding CEO of the Year—widely viewed as the most prestigious award in Canadian business. In 2011, Ed was named Ivey Business Leader of the Year by the Richard Ivey School of Business at the University of Western Ontario. In 2012 and 2013, Ed was named to Barron's prestigious annual list of the World's 30 Best CEOs. *Canadian Business* awarded Ed CEO of the Year in 2013, and in 2014, *American Banker* named Ed a Lifetime Achievement Honoree. In October 2014, the *Harvard Business Review* named Ed to The 100 Top Performing CEOs in the World. In March 2017, Ed received the Canadian Dealmakers Award. Most recently, he was inducted into the Canadian Business Hall of Fame for his "outstanding professional achievements and enduring contributions to Canadian society."

Currently, Ed is Chair of the Vector Institute, an independent non-profit institution dedicated to Artificial Intelligence in fields as diverse as finance, education, environment and clean tech, retail, advanced manufacturing, transportation, and health care.

Ed and his wife Fran make their home in Toronto. They have four grown children and eleven grandchildren.

Fred Tomczyk
Former CEO of TD Ameritrade

Fred Tomczyk is a more than 35-year veteran of the financial services industry with extensive expertise in wealth management, banking, and insurance. His proven leadership style has consistently translated into steady, significant growth for several major financial organizations.

Tomczyk most recently held the role of president and chief executive officer at TD Ameritrade Holding Corporation, from October 2008 to October 2016. He assumed leadership of the company on the eve of the most significant financial crisis to hit the United States since the Great Depression, and in the face of a challenging economic environment, set the company on a successful course for strong organic growth. His legacy includes seven consecutive years of double-digit annualized net new client asset growth, an expanded leadership position in trading and innovation, growth in total client assets from $278 billion to nearly $700 billion, consistent best-in-class employee engagement rates of more than 85 percent, and industry-leading shareholder returns.

Tomczyk started his career with TD Ameritrade as a member of its board of directors following the company's acquisition of TD Waterhouse USA in January 2006. He served as a director from January 2006 until June 2007, when he accepted the role of chief operating officer at the company, responsible for all operations, technology, retail sales functions and the independent registered investment advisor channel. He remained in that role until he became president and chief executive officer and re-joined the board of directors in October 2008.

From May 2002 until joining TD Ameritrade in 2007, Tomczyk served as the vice chair of corporate operations for TD Bank Group ("TD"). From March 2001 until May 2002, he served as executive vice president of retail distribution for TD Canada Trust (a wholly-owned subsidiary of TD), and from September 2000 until March 2001 he served as executive vice president and later as president and chief executive officer of wealth management for TD Bank. Prior to joining TD Bank, he was president and chief executive officer of London Life.

Tomczyk serves on Cornell University's undergraduate business program advisory council. He received a bachelor's degree in applied economic and business management from Cornell University with a Bachelor of Science and subsequently obtained his Chartered Accountant designation. In 2006, he was elected as a Fellow of the Institute of Chartered Accountants of Ontario.

Rose Laboucan, B.Ed, M.Ed
Former Chief at Driftpile First Nation and Grand Chief Lesser Slave Lake Regional Council and Vice Grand Chief Treaty 8

Rose Laboucan is a fierce advocator for strongly educated Aboriginal youth and also advocates on elders, health, and community development. As the first woman chief elected by Driftpile First Nation, she served as Chief for Driftpile First Nation for 12 years and also Grand Chief of Lesser Slave Lake Regional Council and Vice Grand Chief of Treaty 8 Alberta. She was awarded with the prestigious Circle of Honour Award in 2017.

She served on the Assembly of First Nations Education Committee and was their representative for Human Resources and Development. She was also an active member of the Treaty 8 Education Commission and Health Authority.

Laboucan spoke at the Joint Panel review for Enbridge's Northern Gateway pipeline project.

Married for over 30 years, Rose is a proud mother and grandmother.

Randy Findlay, Corporate Director

Randy retired as President and Co-Founder of Provident Energy Trust in 2006. During his time at Provident it grew from a market capitalization of $40M to $4B. His career spanned over 30 years (20 years as an executive) with TransCanada Energy, NOVA and other oil and gas industry companies.

For the last 10 years he has served as a corporate director of public and private companies. He is a director of Pembina Pipeline-TSX, NYSE (board chair), HNZ Group-TSX (past board chair), Superior Plus-TSX, SeaNG Energy-private (board chair), and EllisDon Construction-private. His past directorships include BreitBurn Energy-NYMEX (board chair), Provident Energy-TSX, NYSE, Transalta Power LP-TSX, TransCanada Midstream-private, and Compton Petroleum-TSX NYSE.

He has been a volunteer in the Not For Profit sector for over 20 years including board positions with the Alberta Children's Hospital Foundation (past chair), Hull Child and Family Services Foundation, Alberta Cancer Foundation, Canadian Mental Health Association-Calgary (past chair), and The RESOLVE Campaign to end homelessness in Calgary (vice chair).

He is a founding member of the 30 Percent Club that promotes women as corporate directors.

His involvement at UBC includes: UBC President's Campaign Cabinet, UBC Applied Science Dean's Advisory Council, UBC Alumni Association director, and chair of the UBC Okanagan's Engineering Campaign.

He is the proud recipient of UBC Alumni's Volunteer Leadership Award in 2014. He graduated from UBC in 1973 with a BASc in Chemical Engineering. He was awarded the designation of ICD.D by the Institute of Corporate Directors in 2014.

He is a Lifetime Member of APEGA and a recipient of a Lifetime Achievement Award from the SPE (Society of Petroleum Engineers) and past National Chair (Canada).

Married to Claudia for 45 years they enjoy their 3 children, 5 grand-children, 4 grand-dogs and spend their time between homes in Calgary and Palm Springs.

Cal Yonker
President and CEO, Sierra-Cedar Group
Mr. Yonker is President and Chief Executive Officer of Sierra-Cedar Group, a private company based in Atlanta, Georgia. Sierra-Cedar Group provides IT consulting and managed services across North America and India. Mr. Yonker holds a Masters of Business Administration degree from the Michigan State University and an undergraduate degree from Calvin College.

About the Author

Lorraine A. Moore helps business leaders achieve unprecedented results for organizations and individual leaders.

She has advised organizations in industries as diverse as construction, healthcare, utilities, fintech, retail, technology, energy/oil and gas, financial services, manufacturing, and not-for-profit. Her work takes her throughout North America and Europe. Her global client base includes Enbridge, BHP, Deloitte, Telus, Cofely Fabricom, and others.

Before founding Accelerate Success Group, Lorraine was an executive at TD Bank Financial Group and TransCanada.

Moore holds an MBA, BA, and ICD.D designation. She chaired an advisory committee at Mount Royal University and has been an active board director for over 25 years.

Moore is the author of *Feet to the Fire: How to Exemplify and Create the Accountability that Creates Great Companies.*

Lorraine and her husband are based in Calgary, Canada. She can be reached at www.lorrainemoore.ca.

Index

OTHER TITLES IN THE HUMAN RESOURCE MANAGEMENT AND ORGANIZATIONAL BEHAVIOR COLLECTION

- *Slow Down to Speed Up: Lead, Succeed, and Thrive in a 24/7 World* by Liz Bywater
- *Agile Human Resources: Creating a Sustainable Future for the HR Profession* by Kelly Swingler
- *Infectious Innovation: Secrets of Transforming Employee Ideas Into Dramatic Revenue Growth* by James Allan
- *21st Century Skills for Non-Profit Managers: A Practical Guide on Leadership and Management* by Don Macdonald and Charles Oham
- *Conflict First Aid: How to Stop Personality Clashes and Disputes from Damaging You or Your Organization* by Nancy Radford
- *How to Manage Your Career: The Power of Mindset in Fostering Success* by Kelly Swingler
- *Deconstructing Management Maxims, Volume I: A Critical Examination of Conventional Business Wisdom* by Kevin Wayne
- *Deconstructing Management Maxims, Volume II: A Critical Examination of Conventional Business Wisdom* by Kevin Wayne
- *The Real Me: Find and Express Your Authentic Self* by Mark Eyre
- *Across the Spectrum: What Color Are You?* by Stephen Elkins-Jarrett
- *The Human Resource Professional's Guide to Change Management: Practical Tools and Techniques to Enact Meaningful and Lasting Organizational Change* by Melanie J. Peacock
- *Tough Calls: How to Move Beyond Indecision and Good Intentions* by Linda D. Henman

Announcing the Business Expert Press Digital Library

Concise e-books business students need for classroom and research

This book can also be purchased in an e-book collection by your library as

- a one-time purchase,
- that is owned forever,
- allows for simultaneous readers,
- has no restrictions on printing, and
- can be downloaded as PDFs from within the library community.

Our digital library collections are a great solution to beat the rising cost of textbooks. E-books can be loaded into their course management systems or onto students' e-book readers.
The **Business Expert Press** digital libraries are very affordable, with no obligation to buy in future years. For more information, please visit **www.businessexpertpress.com/librarians**. To set up a trial in the United States, please email **sales@businessexpertpress.com**.

CPSIA information can be obtained
at www.ICGtesting.com
Printed in the USA
LVOW10s2250080518
576468LV00010B/28/P